make your own
own
clothes

20 custom fit patterns to sew

make your own

clothes

20 custom fit patterns to sew

PatternMaker with
Marie Clayton

St. Martin's Griffin
New York

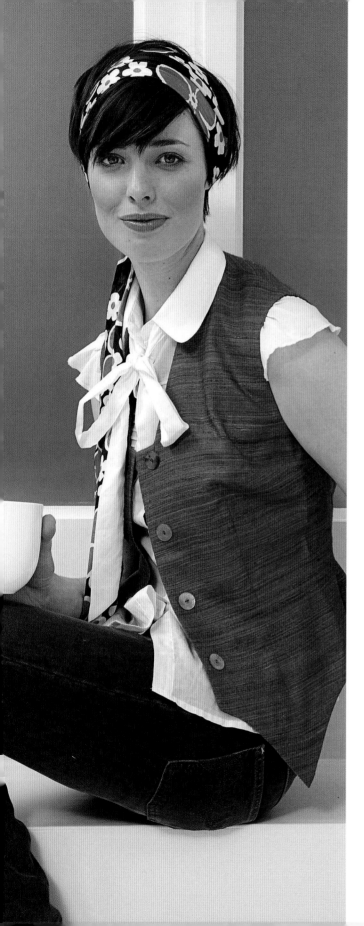

www.stmartins.com

Library of Congress Cataloging-in-Publication Data Available Upon Request

ISBN-13: 978-0-312-37664-2
ISBN-10: 0-312-37664-2

First U.S. Edition: February 2008

10 9 8 7 6 5 4 3 2 1

PatternMaker Software
Pattern Design and Documentation: Leena Lähteenmäki, Thea Botter, Kim Nish
Pattern Tester: Eugenie Naber
Programmers: Gary Pickrell, Lane Holdcroft

Special Thanks to:
Alice & Co and Emily Theodorou for their great sewing, Cadena for supplying the fabrics and Janome for supplying the sewing machine.

Reproduction by Rival Colour Ltd, UK.
Printed in China.

Contents

Seams and gathers

Fitting and fastenings

Sleeves, collars, and pockets

Tailoring techniques

Introduction

One of the great joys of making your own clothes is that you can make garments to fit you exactly, in the fabric of your choice with trimmings that you want. The final result will be unique—even if someone else makes up the same pattern it is unlikely they will pick the exact same fabric or notions as you have. This book is designed to take you through the basics of dressmaking, from the very beginning right through to tailoring techniques to make your garments look professionally finished. Along the way you can make an assortment of stylish projects—and all the patterns you will need are included on the CD and can be printed out at a full range of sizes.

The first chapter covers the basic techniques—here you will learn how to size and cut out patterns, and some simple techniques such as darts, gathering, making a channel for elastic or a drawstring, and seaming and hemming. The projects are all simple to sew so you can build up confidence before moving to the next stage—and they are illustrated with photographs showing key stages of construction so you can compare your garment to make sure it is looking the same. Don't expect perfection the first time—just concentrate on achieving a garment that you can wear. The following chapter builds on skills learned and introduces some new ones. The projects here are a little more shaped and have buttonholes, zippers, and facings.

Chapter three moves on to sleeves, collars, and cuffs, as well as yokes and patch and inset pockets, so patterns are becoming more sophisticated. As before, key stages are illustrated with a photograph so you can see how your work should look. Finally, chapter four is all about tailoring and covers trousers and a range of different jackets—one with a lining.

Getting Started

There are certain basic tools that you will need but, except for a sewing machine, they are not too expensive. Even with the sewing machine you only need a basic model—try out several until you have a feeling for what suits you before purchasing one. To use the CD with this book, which has patterns for all the projects, you will need a PC or PC laptop running Windows 98/NT/2000/XP and 90 MB free disk space, and a windows-compatible printer or plotter. You can also use the Windows partition of a dual-boot MacIntosh computer. See page 28 for further information on loading and running the program.

Equipment

Look through the equipment shown on pages 10–13 to see what you already have and what you may need to buy. You will need a sewing machine, but if you don't have one try to borrow one initially before spending money on buying your own. Pages 14–17 have information on different fabrics to help you make the right choice for your project.

CD software

The CD contains all the patterns you will need to make the projects in this book. You can type in your measurements and print out the pieces at the correct size to fit. For information on loading and running the program on the CD, see page 28.

Basic techniques

Read the techniques pages—although you don't need to learn all of these at the beginning as you can refer back when you need them. The techniques are all numbered, and each time a technique appears in a pattern, the reference number appears in the text as well. Use the fold-out flaps for quick reference to remind you of the technique, or to find out which page has full instructions on how to work it.

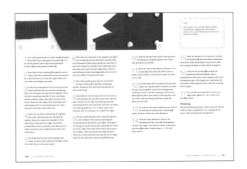

Equipment

Needle threader

This handy device will save time when threading needles.

Sewing thread

Use thread either the same color as your fabric, or a shade darker. If you are using a print fabric, match the thread to the most dominant color. As well as matching the color, try to use the right type of thread for the fabric. Although there are many general-purpose threads, it is generally best to use a cotton thread on most natural fabrics and synthetic thread on man-made fabrics.

Paper scissors

Since the patterns for these projects will be printed out on ordinary printer paper, it is better if you cut the pieces out roughly before pinning them to the fabric. Use a pair of paper scissors for this.

Pins

Pins should be rustproof stainless steel; the type with colored heads are easy to see. Use fine pins for fine fabric to avoid making holes. Keep pins in a plastic box, rather than a metal one that may rust, or in a pincushion where they are always at hand.

Small sharp scissors

These are for snipping threads, clipping into seam allowances and detail work. They should have 3–4 in. (7–10 cm) long pointed blades.

Dressmaker's shears

These scissors have angled handles to allow the blades to rest on the table as you cut the fabric. Choose a pair with a comfortable handle to accommodate all your fingers and that is easy to open and close. The blades should be around 7–8 in. (18–20 cm) long. Invest in a good pair and look after them well— use them only to cut fabric and pattern tissue, never paper as this will quickly blunt the blades.

Needles

There are many different types of sewing needles and the one you choose will depend on the task at hand. For general sewing and most fabrics, medium-length sharps are most useful. For knitted fabric use ballpoint needles as the rounded tips slide between fibers rather than splitting them.

Sewing-machine needles are also available in a range of sizes and with different types of point. Sharp pointed needles are used for woven fabrics, ballpoints for knits, and wedge-shape points for leather.

Tape measure

Choose one that is at least 60 in. (150 cm) long with metal-tipped ends and clearly marked measurements on both sides. The plastic coated type is better because it will not stretch or fray,

Seam ripper

This useful piece of equipment may come with your sewing machine. It is a small cylindrical item with a very sharp curved blade at one end, useful for accurately cutting through stitches and cutting slits for things such as buttonholes.

Pinking shears

These are optional, but they are useful to neaten raw edges on fabrics that do not fray.

Thimble

Although this is not essential for most sewing work, when you are hand-stitching through thick fabric or many layers, it will save your fingers.

Ruler

A plastic transparent ruler is useful for some types of measuring since you can see through it.

Marking tools

There is a wide range of tools available for transferring pattern marks to fabric. Try to mark on the wrong side of the fabric, where possible, so if the marks prove permanent they will not show when the garment is worn. Tailor's chalk comes as a small block or in a pencil, often with a brush at the other end. It is quick and easy to use, and the marks can be brushed away—which sometimes means they wear off before you have finished with them. Air-erasable and water-erasable markers are special marker pens for fabric; the marks they make are a little more permanent but either fade after a certain time or can be removed with water. Be sure to test them on a spare piece of fabric first, just in case the ink proves permanent on the type of fabric you are using. Dressmaker's carbon and a tracing wheel are a good method for transferring lines—the carbon is placed on the fabric with the pattern on top, then the tracing wheel is run along the pattern lines to transfer them. Again, the carbon lines sometimes refuse to shift so test on a scrap of fabric first. Tailor's tacks take a little more time initially, but are suitable for any fabric, stay as long as you need them and are easy to remove.

Sewing Machine

For the projects in this book you will only need a basic machine that can stitch in a straight line and a zigzag. However, other features are always useful—many modern machines have a facility to create a machine-stitched buttonhole automatically and may have a range of simple embroidery stitches. Try a few machines out to see how easy they are to use before buying one.

Gauge

Gauge refers to the amount of pull or tautness on both the needle thread and the bobbin thread in the machine. When it is set correctly, the stitches should be perfectly balanced with the threads interlocking in the center of the fabric so they look the same on both sides. The manufacturer's instructions will tell you how to adjust the gauge of the needle thread—usually by means of a knob on the front of the machine—to correct any problems. Although on some machines it is possible to adjust the bobbin gauge, most manufacturers do not recommend it. Before starting any new project, try out a line of stitching on a scrap piece of the fabric to check the gauge. If you can see the bobbin thread protruding on the right side (RS), the gauge on the needle thread is too high; if the needle thread is showing through on the wrong side (WS), the gauge is too loose.

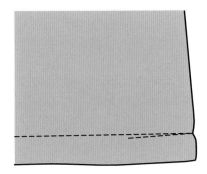

Starting and stopping

If you need to secure the end, insert the needle a little along the seam, set the machine in reverse and make a few backstitches (above) before returning to normal and stitching back over the stitches and down the seam. At the end, put the machine into reverse again and backstitch a little way back. It is difficult to backstitch at the point of a dart, so run the seam off the edge of the fabric before cutting the thread, and then knot the two loose ends.

Sewing a seam

Try a short test seam on a scrap piece of fabric. Using the hand wheel raise the needle to its highest point and pull the needle thread and the bobbin thread to the back or side of the presser foot. Slide the fabric under the presser foot to where you want to begin stitching and lower the foot to hold the fabric in place. Turn the hand wheel to lower the needle into the fabric, then begin stitching, trying to keep a steady, even pace. Guide the fabric in a straight line with one hand gently holding the fabric in the front of the presser foot and the other holding it behind—be careful not to pull the fabric. Watch the edge of the fabric, or a point on the seam you are heading for, rather than the needle—this will help you to sew in a straight line. To keep your seams an even width, align the fabric edge with one of the lines engraved on the presser plate or mark your own with a length of tape.

Stitch length

The length of the stitch can be adjusted on a dial—for normal seams, this should be set at around 2–3. For gathering threads, set the stitch at its longest length, for edge stitching or topstitching, set the stitch to 1–2.

FABRIC SELECTION

There is such a bewildering selection of fiber types, weaves, patterns, and colors available today that it may seem impossible to make a choice. However, some types of fabric are more suitable for dressmaking than others and it will make your life easier if you know what to look for and what not to buy. Always check the laundering instructions on the fabric bolt when you purchase your fabric and choose thread to match the composition of the fabric you will be using.

FABRIC COMPOSITION

Fabrics can be made of natural yarn, man-made yarn or a mixture of the two. Man-made yarns often tend to crease less and can be easier to launder, so they are often added to natural yarns to improve these qualities. Man-made yarns also offer a wide range of possibilities for achieving special effects.

Cotton

Cotton is a natural vegetable yarn made from the soft white fibrous material around the seed of the tropical and subtropical cotton plant. Cotton is almost pure cellulose and in its raw, undyed form is pale or dark cream, brown, or green. It is often classified by its geographical region of origin, hence

Cotton finishes

Cotton is very versatile and can be finished in a wide range of different ways to make it look quite different.

Brushed cotton has been finished with rotating brushes to raise the nap on the surface. It is soft and warm and is often used for nightwear and children's clothes.

Combed cotton is made from yarn that has been combed to remove short fibers and straighten longer fibers to create a smoother, finer thread.

Glazed cotton has a glossy, polished finish but this will be removed after only a few washes, so this fabric is not suitable for most garments and is mainly used for household furnishing projects.

Waterproofed cotton has a treated surface to make it showerproof, although it will not withstand a serious downpour.

Waxed cotton has a waxy coating applied to the outer surface to make it waterproof. This does wear off in time, but garments can be re-waxed professionally.

Egyptian cotton, Indian cotton. Polycotton is made from a mixture of cotton and polyester yarn. Both cotton and linen can be washed easily and cotton and linen blends are quite common.

Linen

Linen is a natural cellulose fiber obtained from the flax plant—its natural color is off-white or tan and due to its wax content it has a natural luster. Linen can be woven in various weights, from very lightweight suitable for handkerchiefs or scarves to heavyweight suit fabrics. Pure linen is cool and comfortable to wear but does crease very easily. Its distinctive crumpled look is often very fashionable, but if this is not required, linen can be blended with other fibers to reduce the possibility of creasing.

Wool

Wool is the fiber or fabric made from the fleece of sheep or lamb—lambs wool is softer and finer. However, the term is also often applied to other animal-hair fibers, including the hair of the camel, alpaca, llama, or vicuña. The wool fleece is spun into yarn, which can be made in various thicknesses. The yarn can then be knitted or woven in fabric. Some types of wool can be washed, but most should be dry-cleaned.

Silk

Silk is a natural filament fiber produced by the silkworm in the construction of its cocoon. Most silk is collected from cultivated worms and comes from Asia. Silk is one of the finest textiles; it is soft, has a brilliant sheen, and is very strong and absorbent, but it can be slippery and hard to sew. Silk takes dye very well and can be hand-printed or even painted to achieve unusual effects and original designs. Silk can also be woven in very lightweight forms that are almost transparent. Some silk can be laundered by hand, but most should be dry-cleaned.

Polyester

A manufactured fiber, made from a group of condensation polymers. It is resilient, smooth, crisp, and particularly springy; it can be shaped with heat and is insensitive to moisture. It is also lightweight, strong, and resistant to creasing, shrinking, and stretching. It is readily washable, is not damaged by sunlight or weather, and is resistant to moths and mildew. Polyester is often combined with other fibers.

Viscose and rayon

Viscose is a man-made fiber made of wood or cotton cellulose treated with sodium hydroxide to make a liquid that can be extruded as cellophane sheet or as viscose rayon yarn. Rayon fiber is very absorbent, dyes well, is soft, and has a good drape. Although it may shrink, it does not melt at high temperature and is resistant to moths, bleach, and household chemicals. Rayon thread is divisible, shiny, and good for blending but is not hardwearing.

Acrylic

Synthetic polymer fabric or yarn, which is lightweight and warm with a wool-like feel. It is resistant to moths, oils, and chemicals, but prone to static and pilling.

Nylon

Developed in 1938, nylon was the first completely synthetic fiber. It is strong and resistant to many chemicals and moths, easy to wash, and non-absorbent.

FABRIC TYPES

Apart from the composition of the fabric, there is also a wide variety of types of fabric available, which differ in the way they are constructed. Some of them are suitable for only a limited range of garment types, others are more suitable for general dressmaking. Some may be difficult to sew and require special handling.

Boiled wool

This is similar to felt and is made from woven wool fabric that has been boiled to thicken it. It is used for hats and structured garments.

Calico

A tightly woven cotton-type fabric with an all-over print, usually a small floral pattern on a contrast background. It is used for dresses, aprons, and quilts. In the UK, this fabric is usually known as sprigged cotton, while calico is a fabric made from unbleached, and often not fully processed, cotton. It is less coarse and thick than canvas or denim, but it is cheap and is often used to make couture garments to test the fit before they are made up in the final fabric. The US term for this fabric is muslin.

Chambray

A cotton fabric that looks like denim but is lightweight. It is a plain-weave fabric with a colored warp and undyed filling yarn. The famous blue working-man's shirt is traditionally made of chambray.

Cheesecloth

A loosely woven undyed cotton used for lightweight clothing.

Chenille

A fuzzy yarn with a pile like a furry caterpillar. It is used mainly for decorative fabrics, embroidery, tassels, and rugs.

Cotton lawn

A very lightweight, plain-weave cotton fabric, often slightly translucent. It is used for blouses, children's clothes, and nightwear.

Corduroy or needle cord

Corduroy is a fabric with ridges of pile (cords) running lengthwise. It is available in various weights and weaves and is used widely for both garments and home furnishings. Needle cord has much finer ridges.

Denim

A rugged, durable twill cotton fabric popular in indigo blue, but also available in paler blue and black. Denim is mainly used for casual garments, such as jeans skirts, and jackets. Denim shrinks when first washed, but most commercial clothing is made of pre-shrunk fabric. Stretch denim has added Lycra®.

Drill

This is a strong, medium- to heavyweight, warp-faced, twill-weave fabric, often made of cotton. It is used for casual trousers and uniforms.

Dupioni

Silk fabric made with yarn from the cocoon of two silkworms that have nested together. The double strand is not separated, so the yarn is uneven and irregular with a large diameter in places and the fabric is plain-weave, very irregular, and shows many slubs.

Felt

Machine-made felt is a non-woven fabric made of compressed wool or acrylic fiber and available in a wide range of colors. It does not fray and can be molded to a shape so it is often used for craft projects and to make hats. Hand-made felt is made from pure wool fleece, which is laid out in a design and then rubbed with warm soapy water to cause the fleece fibers to felt together into a solid mass. Knitted fabrics can be felted by being washed at high temperature then tumble dried.

Fleece

Fleece can be made of acrylic, polyester, or wool, or any combination. It is knitted then brushed to compact the cloth, trap air, and raise the fibers. The surface is then sheared to create a smooth, even finish. Fleece is soft, easy to sew, does not fray, and is available in a wide range of colors and designs. It is warm for its weight and does not hold water, so is ideal for outer garments.

Fur fabric

A man-made fabric with a long 'fur' pile, often colored in imitation of an animal's pelt. Fun fur is similar but made in bright colors and is more obviously artificial. Fur fabric is usually made of acrylic, and is often made into throws, outerwear, or used as a lining or as a trim.

Gabardine

This is a tightly woven, smooth, durable twill-weave fabric with either a lustrous or a dull finish. It comes in various weights and generally wears extremely well, although it is inclined to shine with wear. Wool gabardine is popular as a fabric for tailored suits, coats, and uniforms.

Jersey

A soft, slightly elastic knit fabric mainly used for shirts and dresses. It is ideal for form-fitting designs as it clings to a shape but still drapes well where it falls. Jersey is also made in cotton, wool, or silk.

Metallic fabrics

Lurex® is the registered brand name for a range of metallic yarn and for the fabrics woven in such yarns. Lurex® can have a backing fabric or may be woven without one. It frays very easily and can be difficult to sew. Lamé is a brocade-type fabric, woven with metallic threads, and often used in evening and dress wear and in theatrical and dance costumes. Lamé comes in different varieties, depending on the composition of the other threads in the fabric. Most metallic fabrics require special care when they are cleaned.

Muslin

In the US, the term muslin refers to a coarse cloth, used for sheeting and shirts (see also calico). In the UK, muslin is a smooth, delicately woven cotton fabric, used for dresses and curtains.

Organza

Organza often has a silvery sheen. It creases quite easily, but is easy to iron. It is used for eveningwear and to line items that need stiffening.

Satin

A fabric with a lustrous surface on one side, which is produced by a twill-weave with the weft-threads almost hidden, and a dull back. It is used mainly for lingerie and eveningwear.

Seersucker

A special kind of cotton weave with lines of bunched threads giving alternate stripes of puckered and smooth finish. The stripes always run lengthwise and they are often blue and white—the puckered stripes are colored and the flat ones white. Seersucker is used for blouses, casual shirts, and children's clothing.

Sequined fabrics

A fabric with sequins stitched at regular intervals. It is not ideal for garments that require a lot of structural stitching. Try not to cut through sequins when working.

Tweed

Tweed is a term applied to a range of sturdy fabrics in coarse grades of wool, usually with color effects created by stock-dyed wools, or sometimes in a single color with an interesting weave. The most popular weaves for tweeds are plain, twill, and variations of twill, such as herringbone.

Velvet or velveteen

Velvet is a medium-weight cut-pile fabric woven using two sets of warp yarns to create the upright pile. A luxurious fabric, it is often made with a filament fiber for high luster and smooth handling. Velveteen is a cotton cut-pile fabric woven in the same way.

To Begin

Each of the basic techiques shown here is numbered and the numbers are repeated whenever a technique is specified in a pattern, for quick and easy reference. The fold-out flaps have numbers listed, with the basic diagrams for each technique and the page number to turn to for full instructions. You can use the flaps on the cover just to remind you of the technique, or to help you quickly find the full information on how to work it within these pages.

BASIC TECHNIQUES

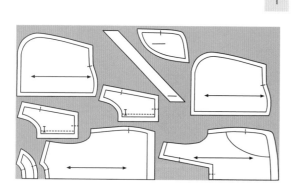

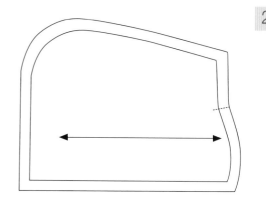

1 Lining up pattern pieces on the straight of grain

Fold the fabric in half lengthwise before you begin. Many pattern pieces will have a straight of grain line marked on them, which must be lined up on the straight of grain of the fabric. Lay the piece out roughly in position on the fabric, then measure from each end of the straight of grain line to the selvedge and adjust the position of the piece until both measurements are the same. Pin along the straight of grain line first to keep the piece lined up before placing other pins.

2 Pinning pattern to fabric

Lay out all the pattern pieces, matching straight of grain lines or placing edges against a fold where required. DO NOT CUT anything until everything is pinned into position, so you are sure you have enough fabric—pieces can often be moved closer together or you can try folding the fabric another way if the first layout does not work. After establishing the straight of grain where necessary, place pins all around the edge of each piece, about 3–4 in. (7.5–10 cm) apart, with a pin set diagonally at each corner for stability.

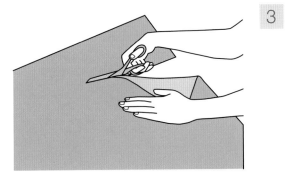

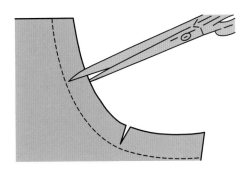

3 Cutting out

When cutting out the pattern pieces, keep the bottom blade of the shears flat on the cutting surface as much as possible—try not to lift the fabric up too much—and keep the blades at right angles to the fabric. Move forward as evenly as possible. When cutting a straight line, look at a point you are aiming for rather than watching the blades cut—this will help keep your line straight. DO NOT CUT along fold lines—when the edge of a pattern piece is laid on the fold it is because the final piece needs to open out into one piece of fabric with each side a mirror image of the other. When cutting other edges, just follow the outer cutting line—the inner line indicates the stitching line of the seam and the difference between the two is called the seam allowance.

4 Marking notches

Notches appear on some edges of pattern pieces, projecting out from the cutting line—they indicate where pattern pieces must be matched together at seams. Transfer them to the fabric pieces by cutting out round them so your fabric piece also has a protruding notch—you can cut these off after the seam is stitched for a neater finish.

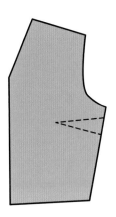

5 Marking darts, buttonholes, and other details

There are certain features marked on the pattern pieces that must be transferred to the fabric pieces. Be sure to transfer any dots, lines that indicate a fold line, pocket and buttonhole positions, center front and center back lines, and lines or dots indicating darts, tucks, or pleats. You do not need to transfer the straight of grain lines or the seam allowance line.

TIP

- *You can use tailor's tacks, a fabric marker, tailor's chalk or a tracing wheel and carbon to mark lines on the fabric. Make sure your chosen method will last as long as you need it and test markers on a spare piece of fabric to make sure the marks will erase when no longer needed.*

BASIC STITCHES

There are several basic machine- and hand-stitches that you will use again and again in all the projects in the book.

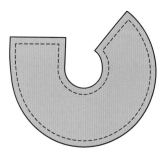

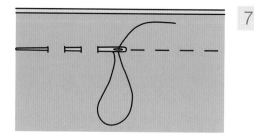

6 Stay-stitching

Curved and bias edges can stretch out of shape before final stitching. Stay-stitching can be used to stabilize edges. With a stitch length of 2–3, stitch a single line within the seam allowance, on all curved or bias cut edges. Stitch in the direction of the fabric weave—run your finger along the cut edge; it will be smoother in one direction and that is the direction in which to stitch.

7 Basting/tacking

To match pieces accurately, it is best to stitch them roughly together first before sewing the final seam. This can be done by hand or by machine, although hand-stitching can be much easier to remove when no longer needed. In either case, use a long stitch and do not secure the ends. You can also pin pieces together before seaming, but this method is less secure on complex joins.

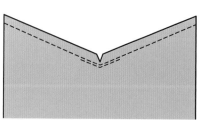

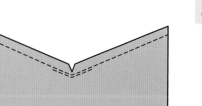

8 Reinforcement stitching

Trimmed corners and curved seams which are clipped may come under strain. To secure these areas, either shorten the stitch length as you come to those areas or run a second line of stitching immediately over the first line.

9 Gathering – set the stitch to long, then stitch two rows within the seam allowance 1/4 in. (6 mm) apart, leaving long ends of thread. Pin RS together, matching notches. Gently pull the bobbin threads, sliding the fabric until it fits then even the gathers. Stitch with the gathered side uppermost, being careful not to pull the gathers as you sew.

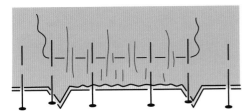

10 Ease stitching

This is used to join a longer edge to a slightly shorter one. It is similar to gathering but there should be no visible folds on the right side after the seam is stitched. With the stitch set on its longest length, run a single line of stitching along the edge to be eased, just inside the seam line. With RS together, pin the longer edge to the shorter edge, matching notches, seams and markings. Gently pull the bobbin threads at each end, distributing the fullness evenly.

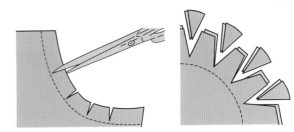

11 Clipping and notching

Make curved seams lie flat. On inward or concave curves, make little clips or snips in the seam allowance just up to—but not through—the line of stitching. On outward or convex curves, cut wedge-shaped notches from the seam allowance to eliminate excess fullness.

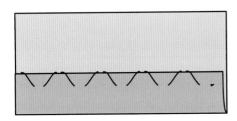

12 Hemming

This is a hand-stitching technique used for all types of hemming, particularly on unlined garments or finished with seam binding. Secure the sewing thread at a seam. Take an inconspicuous stitch in the garment, and then bring the needle diagonally up through the edge of the seam binding or hem edge. Space the stitches about 1/4 in. (6 mm) apart.

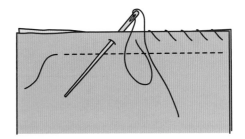

13 Overcasting

This hand-stitching technique is also known as oversewing. It is used to finish raw edges and is worked by inserting the needle at an angle, from the back to the front, usually working through a single piece of fabric.

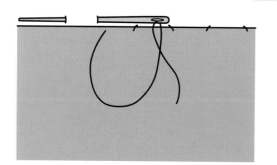

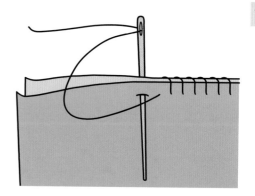

14 Slipstitch

This hand-stitching technique is used for securing cuffs and waistbands and other turned-under edges. The stitches are invisible on both the inside and the outside of the garment. Fasten the thread to the folded edge of the fabric. Working right to left, pick up a single fabric thread just below the folded edge. Insert the needle into the fold directly above the first stitch and bring it out 1/4 in. (6 mm) away. Pick up another thread in the garment directly below the point where the needle emerged and continue, alternating between garment and fold.

15 Whipstitch

This hand-stitching technique joins two edges together or holds a facing in place by attaching it to a seam allowance. The needle is inserted from back to front, at right angles to the finished edges. The distance between the stitches can vary according to the task—for joining edges, the stitches should be no more than 1/4 in. (6 mm) apart maximum, but for holding a facing in place, space them further apart.

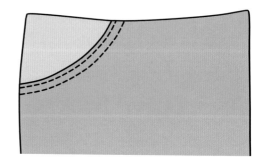

16 Topstitching

This is an extra row of stitching on the outside of a garment along or near a finished edge. Although topstitching is usually decorative, it can be functional; it may be used to attach a patch pocket or insert a zipper. Use a matching or a contrasting thread and stitch with a small- to medium-length stitch.

TIPS

- *When gathering very long edges there is a risk that the bobbin thread may break, so divide the length into equal parts and do each as a separate section.*

- *Stitch gathers with the gathered side uppermost, so you don't pull the gathers out of place with the feed dog as you sew.*

BUTTONHOLE TECHNIQUES

Your sewing machine may well have an automatic program to stitch a buttonhole, in which case follow the instructions in the manufacturer's handbook. The bound buttonhole is useful for tailored garments and the hand-stitched buttonhole adds an individual touch when it is done well.

17 Machine-stitched buttonhole

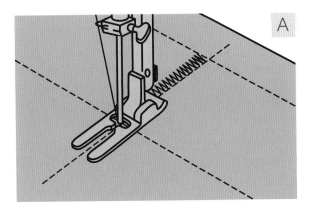

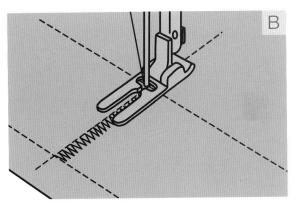

A. Following your sewing machine instruction book, position the sewing machine needle to the left of center and use a close zigzag stitch set at half width to stitch along one side of the buttonhole.

B. At the end of this side, lower the needle into the fabric on the RS. Lift the presser foot and pivot the fabric around. Lower the presser foot, lift the needle, and make a few stitches at full width to form an end bar, ending with the needle at the outer edge of the buttonhole.

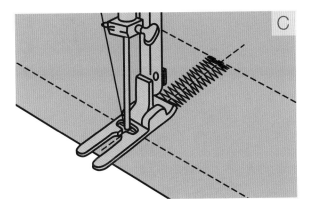

C. Lift the needle, re-set the stitch width to half and stitch the other side of the buttonhole. Finish with full width stitches to form an end bar, as before.

> ### TIP
>
> - *When you mark your buttonhole, check the length against the button you plan to use. Try out the button in the first buttonhole finished—if it is too big you can stitch across the end to shorten it, while if it is too small you can remake just one and make the remaining ones bigger.*

18 Bound buttonhole

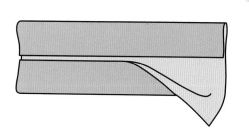

A

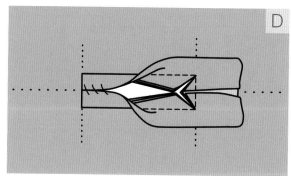

B

A. Mark the position of the buttonhole precisely. Cut a piece of garment fabric 1 in. (2.5 cm) wide and 1 in. (2.5 cm) longer than the buttonhole. With WS together, fold the long edges so the raw edges meet in the center.

B. With the cut edges facing up, center the patch over the buttonhole markings on the RS. Tack through the center. Using small stitches, start at the center of one lip and stitch a rectangular box around the buttonhole marking, working the same number of stitches across each end and pivoting at the corners. Do not finish with backstitches but pull the ends to the WS and tie off.

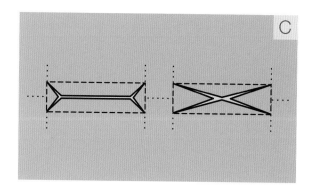

C

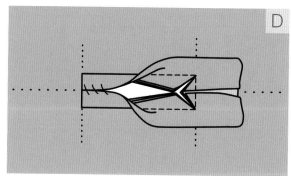

D

C. Remove the tacking and slash through the center of the patch and the garment, between the rows of stitching, clipping diagonally into the corners. There are two methods of slashing the opening. Either cut along the center to within 1/4 in. (6 mm) of each end, then clip diagonally into the corners. Alternatively, for fabrics that fray, cut from the center diagonally into each corner. With either method, take care NOT to cut the stitches.

D. Turn the patch through to the WS and tack the folds together along the center, then press.

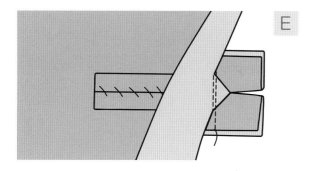

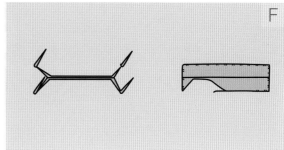

E. With the garment RS up, fold the garment back and stitch back and forth over the little triangles at each end. Trim the patch to 1/4 in. (6 mm) from the stitching line.

F. To finish the buttonhole on the inside, the facing will need a matching hole. With the facing in position, push a pin through each corner of the buttonhole. Slash the facing along the center line of the buttonhole and clip diagonally into the corners. Turn the raw edges under and slipstitch in place.

19 Hand-stitched buttonhole

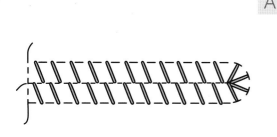

A. Using small stitches, machine a rectangle 1/8 in. (3 mm) around the buttonhole position line. Slash along the position line and oversew the raw edges.

B. A horizontal buttonhole has fanned stitches at the end toward the fabric edge; a vertical one has a bar tack at each end. These instructions are for a horizontal buttonhole. With the fanned edge of the buttonhole to the right, fasten matching buttonhole thread to the bottom left corner, then working from left to right, insert the needle through the slash to the RS just outside the line of machine-stitching. Loop the thread under the point and the eye of the needle. Pull the needle to form a small knot at the cut edge—this is known as buttonhole stitch.

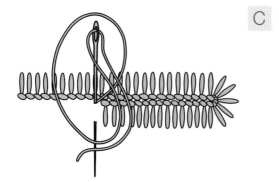

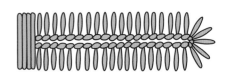

C. Working stitches close together, continue along the edge. At the end, fan the stitches then turn around and work along the other edge.

D. At the final end work several long stitches across the two rows of buttonhole stitches—known as a bar tack—then fasten off.

20 Sewing on a button

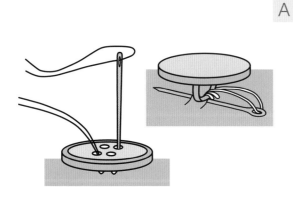

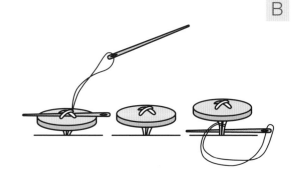

A. Some buttons have a loop or shank on the back, which you sew through to attach the button and which holds it above the surface of the fabric to allow for the thickness of the upper fabric layer. Other buttons must be stitched through the holes provided and may require a thread shank.

B. To make a thread shank, place a matchstick or toothpick on top of the button and sew over it. Remove the stick, lift the button, and wind the thread around the extra length of thread between the button and the garment. Bring the needle to the underside of the garment and fasten with several small stitches.

SEAM TECHNIQUES

Simple plain seams are fine for most situations, but there are a couple of special seams it is useful to be able to do. The French seam adds a couture look to the inside of a garment and is perfect for sheers and other lightweight fabrics. The flat fell seam is a sturdy seam—often used on jeans and heavy fabrics.

21 French seam

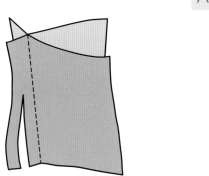

A. With WRONG SIDES together, stitch the seam only 1/2 in. (12 mm) from the edge. Trim the seam allowance to a scant 1/8 in. (3 mm) and press open.

B. Fold the fabric RS together along the stitching line you have just made. Stitch a second seam on the seam line, enclosing the raw edges of the fabric. From the WS, press the seam to one side.

22 Flat fell seam

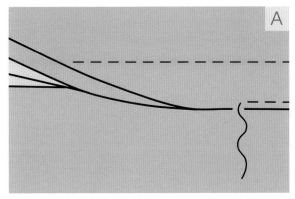

A. With WRONG SIDES together, stitch the seam 1/2 in. (12 mm) from the edge. Trim the seam allowance on one side to 1/8 in. (3 mm) and press this side open.

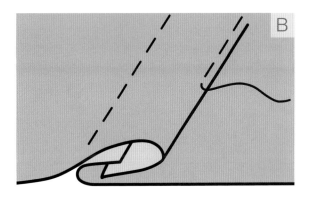

B. Turn under 1/4 in. (6 mm) of the untrimmed seam allowance and tack in place on the RS of the garment over the trimmed edge. Edge stitch close to the fold, through seam allowance and garment.

Using the CD

The CD supplied with this book has patterns for all the projects. You will need a PC or PC laptop running Windows 98/NT/2000/XP and 20 MB free disk space, and a Windows-compatible printer or plotter. You can also use the Windows partition of a dual-boot MacIntosh computer. Load the CD onto your computer—it should start straight away, but if not click on the Make Your Own Clothes icon to upload the program. The password you need to enter is custompats. Enter it exactly as shown here and please keep disk and book together as PatternMaker will not issue the password again. The disk allows you to print out each pattern in a size to suit whoever the garment is for, but before trying this out please read the PDF files on the CD "How to run a macro" and "How to measure."

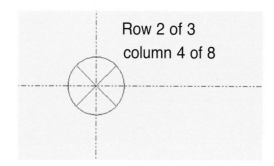

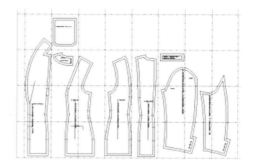

Printing the patterns

The patterns can be printed out in sections on any size paper that your printer will take, but you will probably need to paste several sheets together to get the full pattern. After you have selected your pattern and the size you need, the pattern pieces required will appear as outlines on the screen. You can move these outlines around on the screen before printing them out so that each one is made up of as few pieces of paper as possible. Each sheet will have matching points printed on each corner—just line these up and tape the sheets together to get your pattern pieces, then cut each pattern piece out roughly before pinning it to the fabric.

Cutting layout and fabric amounts

The program on the disk allows you to type in the width of the fabric you want to use and then lay out the pattern pieces on screen to fit them into a length of fabric. Note that some pieces need to be placed to a fold line along one edge—this is noted on the pattern piece itself, and on the diagram and list of pattern pieces at the beginning of each pattern in the book. When you are happy with your layout you can print it out to follow when pinning the pieces to the fabric—the box at the top of the screen will also tell you how much fabric you will need to buy for your layout.

CD TIPS

- Cut the pattern pieces from a double thickness of fabric by folding the fabric in half down its length before positioning the pattern pieces on top. Some pieces just need to be placed on the straight of grain, so you cut two separate pieces, others need to have one edge on a fold so you cut one piece with a fold down the center.

- Note that the program automatically adds a seam allowance all round the pattern. On edges that are to be placed to a fold line, you will need to trim the seam allowance off this edge ONLY and place the SEAM LINE to the fold. Edges to be placed to a fold are noted on each relevant piece, as well as on the diagram and list of pieces at the beginning of each pattern in the book.

- Until you are confident in using the CD and get the hang of doing your own pattern layouts, buy an extra 1/4 yd (25 cm) or so more fabric than indicated by the program so you have some spare for errors.

- Be careful to avoid stretching the tape when taking your measurements; check each measurement three times!

- Print out the measurement chart on the CD to record your measurements—they cannot be saved in the program.

- The patterns can be printed on any size paper your printer can take, but try to use the largest size possible to save on paper and the number of taped joins needed.

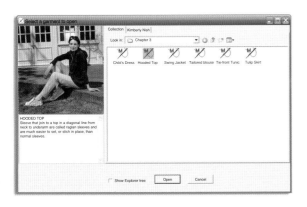

1
Seams and gathers

This chapter covers all the basics of making your own clothes: how to lay out and cut out patterns, basic seams, simple waist darts, and making a channel for elastic or a drawstring. It also covers some finishing techniques and hemming. The projects are very simple and require little fitting—just concentrate on learning the skills and creating a garment that you can wear.

Wrap Skirt

This is an ideal project on which to learn to sew; the shape is simple and the skirt wraps around and fastens at the waist with snap fasteners. There are no zippers or buttonholes to worry about—the buttons on the waistband are just for show.

Pattern pieces

A. Front wrap—cut two in fabric

B. Back—place center back line to a fold, cut one in fabric

C. Waistband—cut two in fabric, two in interfacing

Suitable fabrics

Lightweight cotton, polycotton, fine wool, polyester

Notions

Sewing thread to match fabric

Interfacing for waistband

Three medium-size snap fasteners

Two decorative buttons

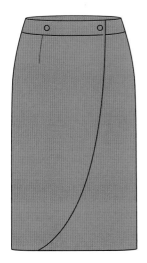

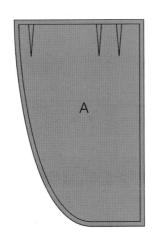

A

B

C

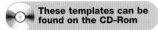

These templates can be found on the CD-Rom

1 Line up the pattern pieces on the straight of grain of the fabric ① and pin them in position ②. Cut out ③ all the pattern pieces as listed and mark notches ④ and the position of darts ⑤.

2 Run a line of stay-stitching ⑥ along the curved edges of the two front sections to keep the edges stable and stop them stretching as you work.

3 Fold the fabric RS together along the center of each dart at the top of each section of the skirt, matching dots, and baste ⑦ in place. Stitch the darts.

4 Place the back section and one front section RS together, matching the notches on the side seam, and pin or baste ⑦ together. Stitch the side seam.

5 Repeat step 4 for the other side seam, then from the WS, press both side seams open and finish the raw edges with a zigzag machine stitch to stop them fraying.

6 To make a baby hem, machine-stitch 1/8 in. (3 mm) in from the raw edge of the fabric all along the RS of the curved edge of the overwrap, right around the hem of the back of the skirt, and up the curved edge of the underlap. Press the fabric under along the stitching line, so the raw edge is pointing upward on the WS. On the RS, machine-stitch 1/8 in. (3 mm) in from the edge of the fold all around again. Press under along the new stitching

line, so the raw edge on the WS is now enclosed. On the RS, topstitch ⑯ as close as possible to the edge of the hem all around to hold all the folds on the WS in place.

7 Join the two pieces of the waistband together along one short end and place the strips of interfacing on the WS, overlapping slightly at the joining seam. Baste ⑦ the interfacing in position with large stitches that will be easy to remove later. Fold the waistband/tie in half along the length where marked, RS together, and press the fold.

8 Open out the waistband again and place it RS together along one long edge to the top edge of the skirt, matching center back line, all notches, and raw edges, and baste ⑦ in place. The waistband should extend beyond the skirt at both ends by 5/8 in. (15 mm). Stitch the waistband to the skirt through one side only. Press the seam upward toward the waistband.

9 Press the waistband upward along the seam line, then fold it back down RS together lengthwise along the center fold line. Stitch across each end from the fold to the lower seam line, being careful not to catch the skirt. Trim the seam allowance.

10 Turn the waistband RS out, enclosing the raw edges of both skirt and waistband, tuck the seam allowance under on the inside, and press.

6

7

10

11

11 Stitch the inside of the waistband into place all round with topstitching ⑯, making sure to keep the line of stitching straight and evenly spaced from the edge.

12 Stitch one half of each of two snap fasteners on the overlap edge of the waistband, near the edge. Try the skirt on and check where the overlap extends to, then stitch the other half of each snap fastener in place on the underlap of the waistband. Sew the remaining snap fastener to the end of the underlap and the corresponding position on the inside of the waistband.

13 Sew on a button ⑳ on the RS of the overlap above the snap fasteners, and a second button, positioned to match, on the other side of the front waistband.

Finishing

Remove all basting threads. Neaten any loose thread ends by either sewing them in or snipping them close to the stitching. Press the garment.

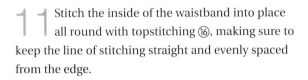

TIPS

- When stitching darts, always work from the edge of the fabric toward the point of the dart.

- Use medium-size snap fasteners with a strong grip—the smaller ones may not be strong enough to hold the skirt wrap firmly closed as you move around.

Basic Pants

A pair of easy-fit pants with an elasticized waistband are comfortable to laze around in. This design is a cinch to make and features no shaping. Add a simple patch pocket to the front or the back.

Pattern pieces

A. Front section—cut two in fabric

B. Back section—cut two in fabric

C. Waistband—place center back line to a fold, cut one in fabric

Suitable fabrics

Lightweight cotton, polycotton, fine wool, polyester

Notions

Sewing thread to match fabric

1 yd. (1 m) of 1 in. (2.5 cm) wide elastic

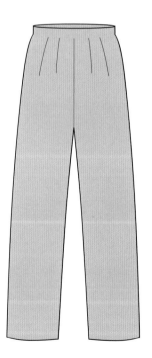
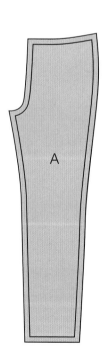
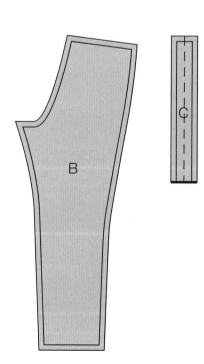

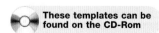

These templates can be found on the CD-Rom

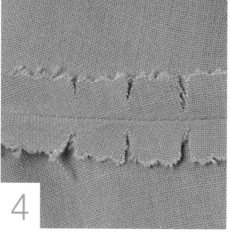

3

4

8

1 Line up the pattern pieces on the straight of grain of the fabric ① and pin them in position ②. Cut out all the pattern pieces ③ as listed and mark notches ④ and the position of darts ⑤.

2 Run a line of stay-stitching ⑥ along the curved edges of the crotch on all four main sections to keep the edges stable and stop them stretching as you work.

3 Place the two front sections RS together, matching notches, and baste ⑦ in place. Stitch the center front seam.

4 Make a series of little clips ⑪ into the seam allowance on the curved crotch seam, being very careful not to cut into the stitching . Space them about 1 in. (2.5 cm) apart, so that the curved seam will lie flat. From the WS, press the seams open.

5 Place the two back sections RS together, matching notches, and baste ⑦ in place. Stitch the center back seam. Clip ⑪ into the seam allowance on the curved crotch seam as before, being very careful not to cut into the stitching. From the WS, press the seams open.

6 Place the back and front sections RS together, matching notches, and baste ⑦ in place. Stitch the side seams. From the WS, press the seams open and either trim them with pinking shears or zigzag

along the raw edges to stop them fraying. Turn the pants RS out.

7 Fold the waistband in half widthwise along the center front, RS together, and stitch partway across the short end, stopping around 1 1/2 in. (4 cm) from the edge. Open out the waistband into a circle of fabric and press the seam allowance open across the full width of the waistband.

8 Place the unbroken circular edge of the waistband RS together to the top of the trousers, matching center back line and all notches. Pin together and then baste ⑦ in place.

9 Stitch the waistband and the trousers together right round the top. Press the seams toward the waistband, then fold the waistband over to enclose the seam you have just made. Press the seam allowance upward on the inside of the waistband and slipstitch ⑭ in place all around. On the inside of the waistband there will be a small vertical opening where the seam joining the two ends of the waistband together was not stitched all the way across in step 7.

10 Cut a length of elastic to fit around your waist loosely, allowing an extra 1 in. (2.5 cm) as an overlap so you can stitch the ends together. Pin a large safety pin to one end of the elastic and pin the other end to the waistband near the vertical hole

10

11

13

left in the seam. Thread the end of the elastic into the hole in the waistband and use your fingers to ease the safety pin all through the channel.

11 When both ends of the elastic are protruding from the hole in the waistband, overlap them and pin together. Check the elastic is flat all round the waistband and not twisted anywhere before stitching the ends together. To secure, stitch a square box with two diagonal lines, as shown, rather than simply stitching one line across the double thickness of elastic.

12 Slipstitch ⑭ the opening in the waistband to close it.

13 Try the pants on to check the length before turning the hem, or measure them against an existing pair the right length. Mark the hemline and press around the bottom of each leg, pinning the hem in position; try the pants on again to check the length is correct. Fold under 1/4 in. (6 mm) seam allowance along the raw edge, then machine-stitch around each leg end.

Finishing

Remove all basting threads. Neaten any loose thread ends by either sewing them in or snipping them close to the stitching. Press the garment.

TIPS

- *Do not pull the elastic tight to your waist when measuring the length to cut, or the waistband will cut in and be uncomfortable when the trousers are worn.*

- *As you get near the end of the channel when threading elastic into the waistband, it is easy for the other end to slip into the hole and be lost, so you have to begin again. To prevent this happening, try pinning the free end to the fabric near the hole before you start threading.*

Drawstring Shorts

This summer-time essential keeps you cool when temperatures rise. Featuring a drawstring waistband, the shorts are designed to be mid-thigh length, but could be made shorter or longer by removing or adding length to the pattern before laying it out on the fabric.

Pattern pieces

A. Leg piece—cut two in fabric

B. Waistband—place center back line to a fold, cut one in fabric

Suitable fabrics

Lightweight cotton, polycotton, fine wool, chambray

Notions

Sewing thread to match fabric

1 yd. (1 m) of narrow cord for the drawstring

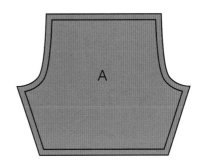

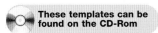

These templates can be found on the CD-Rom

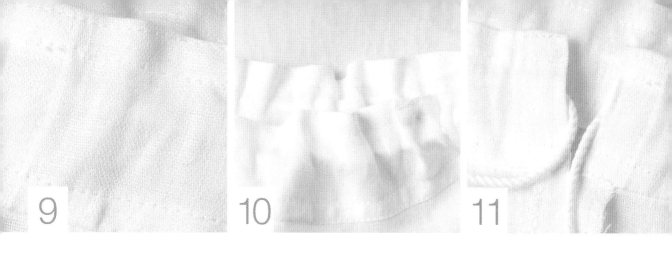

9   10   11

1 Line up the pattern pieces on the straight of grain of the fabric ① and pin them in position ②. Cut out all the pattern pieces ③ as listed and mark notches ④ and the position of darts ⑤.

2 Run a line of stay-stitching ⑥ along the curved edges of the crotch on both sides of both main sections to keep the edges stable and stop them stretching as you work.

3 Place the two sections RS together, matching notches, and baste ⑦ in place. Stitch the crotch seams. Make a series of little clips ⑪ into the seam allowance on the curved crotch seam, being very careful not to cut into the stitching. Space them about 1 in. (2.5 cm) apart, so that the curved seam will lie flat.

4 From the WS, press the seams open.

5 Place the two leg sections RS together, matching notches, and baste ⑦ in place. Stitch the leg seams. From the WS, press the seams open and zigzag along the raw edges to stop them fraying. Turn the shorts RS out.

6 Fold each short end of the waistband under by 1/4 in. (4 mm) and press. Then fold the waistband in half lengthway, RS together, and press. Open out again and place one long edge along the waistline of the shorts, RS together and matching side seams and all notches. The two short folded-under ends of the waistband need to be at center front, as they will be opening the drawstring. Pin together then baste ⑦ in place.

7 Stitch the waistband and shorts together right round the top. Fold the waistband over to enclose the seam you have just made, pin, and slipstitch ⑭ in place on the inside.

8 Run a line of topstitching ⑯ around the waistband 1/8 in. (3 mm) from the top edge, another 1/4 in. (6 mm) away, and a third line 1/8 in. (3 mm) from the bottom edge.

9 Use a bodkin—a needle with a very large eye to take wide ribbon or string—to thread the drawstring.

10 Thread the end of the drawstring into the slit left in the front of the waistband and use your fingers to ease the bodkin or safety pin all through the channel.

11 When both ends of the drawstring are protruding from the hole in the waistband, adjust them to an equal length on both sides. Finish the ends of the drawstring with a neat knot, or add a purchased toggle end, following the instructions to fix it to the drawstring.

12 Try the shorts on to check the length before turning the hem, or measure them against an existing pair the right length. Press and pin the hem in place and try them on again to check the length is correct before hemming ⑫ or machine-stitching around each leg end.

Finishing

Remove all basting threads. Neaten any loose thread ends by either sewing them in or snipping them close to the stitching. Press the garment.

TIP

- If the fabric you have choosen is not wide enough when folded to cut the two shorts pieces at the same time from a double layer of fabric, you can cut each piece individually from a single thickness instead. Read the PDF file section 5.3 "Cut 4" on the CD to learn how to calculate the extra fabric that will be required for this.

Beret

Get a head start with this easy-going beret in water-repellent fleece. The shape may look daunting, but it's easy to create with just three simple seams.

Pattern pieces

A. Top—cut one in fabric

B. Side band—cut one in fabric

C. Edging strip—place center front line to a fold, cut one in fabric, one in interfacing

Suitable fabrics

Fleece, felt, boiled wool, jersey, heavyweight velvet

Notions

Sewing thread to match fabric

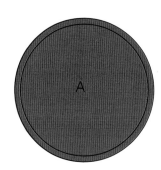
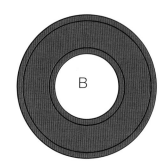

These templates can be found on the CD-Rom

3

5

7

1 Line up the pattern pieces on the straight of grain of the fabric ① and pin them in position ②. Cut out all the pattern pieces ③ as listed and mark notches ④.

2 Run a line of stay-stitching ⑥ along the curved edges of the top to keep it stable and stop it stretching as you work.

3 Place the side band and the top RS together, and pin and baste ⑦ in place round the outside of the circle. Stitch round the seam. Make a series of little clips ⑪ into the seam allowance on the curved seam, being very careful not to cut into the stitching. Space them about 1 in. (2.5 cm) apart, so that the curved seam will not be bulky. Alternatively, if you have used a fabric that will not fray, trim the seam with pinking shears, being careful not to go too close to the line of stitching.

4 From the WS, press the seam open—although the seam will not lie open, pressing it flat will neaten the seam line on the RS of the fabric. Turn the beret RS out.

5 Baste the interfacing to the WS of the edging strip, then trim back so it is ¼ in. (6 mm) smaller. Fold the edging strip in half widthwise, RS together, matching notches, and stitch the ends together to make a circle. Press the seam flat.

6 Open out the edging strip into a circle and refold it along the center fold line, WS together, to make a circular band of fabric with RS outward.

7 With the beret RS out, ease the side band of the beret inside the circle of the edging strip, with RS together, all three raw edges in line, and matching any notches. Pin and baste ⑦ in place, then stitch around the seam.

8 Press the seam toward the beret, then fold the edging strip downward.

Finishing

Remove all basting threads. Neaten any loose thread ends by either sewing them in or snipping them close to the stitching.

> **TIP**
> * When sewing velvet or other fabric with a pile, the pile can sometimes get caught in the seam and make the join look more obtrusive. If this happens, gently tease the caught threads out with the point of a needle.

2

Fitting and fastenings

From a shapely vest to a sophisticated dress, the styles within this chapter are designed with maximum appeal. Build on skills already learned and discover how to make buttonholes, insert zippers, and add facings to give your garments more structure.

Scoop-neck Top

This elegant top is a basic shape that is quite figure hugging, so you can check how the rest of the patterns in the book will fit. If it doesn't fit you perfectly, read the PDF file section 2.1 "How to measure" on the CD to see what measurements you need to change to put things right.

Pattern pieces

A. Front—place center front line to a fold, cut one in fabric

B. Side front—cut two in fabric

C. Side back—cut two in fabric

D. Center back—cut two in fabric

E. Sleeve—cut two in fabric

Suitable fabrics

Lightweight cotton, cotton lawn, polycotton, muslin

Notions

Sewing thread to match fabric

One 22 in. (56 cm) zipper

Bias binding in a color to match the fabric (optional)

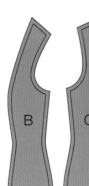

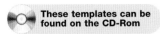

These templates can be found on the CD-Rom

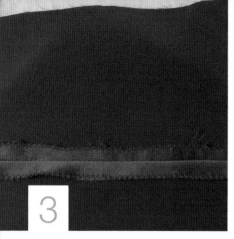

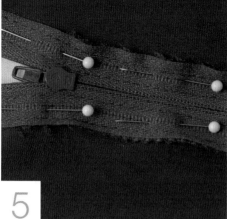

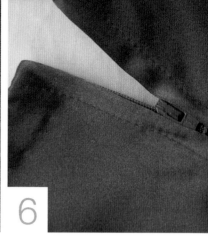

3

5

6

1 Line up the pattern pieces on the straight of grain of the fabric ① and pin them in position ②. Cut out all the pattern pieces ③ as listed and mark notches ④ and the position of darts ⑤.

2 Run a line of stay-stitching ⑥ along the curved edges of the front and back sections and around the top of the sleeves to keep the edges stable and stop them stretching as you work.

3 Place the front and one side front RS together and stitch the princess seam, which runs down the front from shoulder to hem. From the WS, press the seam open and zigzag stitch to finish the edges.

4 Repeat step 3 for the other side front.

5 Place the two back pieces RS together and baste ⑦ the center back seam. Stitch the center back seam from the base of the back to the mark indicating the base of the zipper, then from the WS, press the seam allowance open. With WS uppermost, center the closed zipper over the seam allowance, with the reverse of the zipper facing upward and the end stopper lined up with the mark indicating the base of the zipper.

6 On the RS of the garment, topstitch ⑯ along each side of the zipper, parallel to the center seam and around 1/4 in. (6 mm) away from it

(depending on the width of the zipper selvedge edges). Be careful to keep the seam running straight as you go past the zipper pull.

7 With RS together, stitch the fronts to the back along the side seams, then stitch the shoulder seams. From the WS, press the seams open.

8 Stitch the dart in the elbow of the sleeve. With RS together, stitch the sleeve seam to make a tube of fabric. From the WS, press the seam open.

9 Turn the sleeve RS out and turn the garment inside out. Slip the sleeve inside the armhole and pin them together at the sleeve and garment underarm seams, shoulder markings and notches. Baste ⑦ into place, then stitch on the machine with the sleeve side up, being careful not to pull the fabric as you work.

10 To reinforce the seam under the arm, stitch a second line of reinforcement stitching ⑧ inside the first, within the seam allowance.

11 Trim the seam allowance close to the stitching and clip curves ⑪, then zigzag or overcast the edges. Repeat steps 8–11 for the other sleeve.

12 Cut a strip of fabric 5/8 in. (15 mm) wide on the bias—so it is stretchy—and long enough to go around the neckline. With RS together, stitch

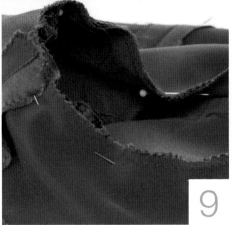

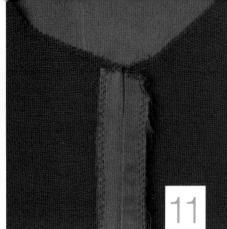

this strip around the neckline, then fold it over to the inside of the neckline and hem ⑫ in place, tucking in the raw edges neatly at each end.

13 Turn under the seam allowance around the ends of the sleeves to a suitable length. Turn the raw edges under again by at least ¼ in. (6 mm) and machine-stitch around the sleeve ends.

14 Turn up the hemline to a suitable length, following the same instructions as for the sleeve ends (see step 13), and either hem ⑫ or machine-stitch in place.

Finishing

Remove all basting threads. Neaten any loose thread ends by either sewing them in or snipping them close to the stitching. Press the garment, then try it on to check the fit.

TIP

- *Tailor's tacks are marks made in thread used to transfer symbols from the pattern to the fabric. Take a small stitch through the pattern mark and both thicknesses of fabric, then take a second in the same place, leaving a large loop of thread on one side. Cut the thread end and snip through the end of the loop, then remove the pattern. Ease the layers of fabric apart and snip through the threads between them, leaving a few strands to mark the place in each piece of fabric.*

Sleeveless Dress

This sleek dress is a staple for any wardrobe—make it in lightweight cotton as a pretty sundress or in a heavier fabric for spring and fall. It could also be made as a simple but sophisticated evening dress.

Pattern pieces

A. Front—place center front line to a fold, cut one in fabric

B. Side front—cut two in fabric

C. Side back—cut two in fabric

D. Center back—cut two in fabric

E. Pleat underlay—cut one in fabric

F. Back neck facing—cut two in fabric, two in interfacing

G. Front neck facing—place center front line to a fold, cut one in fabric, one in interfacing

H. Front armhole facing—cut two in fabric, two in interfacing

I. Back armhole facing—cut two in fabric, two in interfacing

Suitable fabrics

Cotton, polycotton, linen, fine wool

Notions

Sewing thread to match fabric

Interfacing for facings

One 22 in. (56 cm) zipper

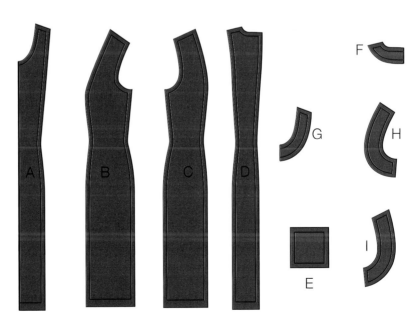

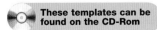
These templates can be found on the CD-Rom

1 Line up the pattern pieces on the straight of grain of the fabric ① and pin them in position ②. Cut out all the pattern pieces ③ as listed and mark notches ④.

2 Run a line of stay-stitching ⑥ along the curved edges of all the front and back sections to keep the edges stable and stop them stretching as you work.

3 Place one side front piece RS together to the front, matching notches. Pin and baste ⑦ along the sewing line, then stitch the seam from top to bottom.

4 Repeat step 3 for the side front. From the WS, press the seams flat toward the side seams.

5 Place one of the back sections and one of the back side sections RS together matching notches. Pin and baste ⑦ along the sewing line, then stitch the seam from top to bottom. Repeat on the other back section.

6 Place the two back pieces RS together and baste ⑦ the center back seam then machine-stitch from the notch marking the end of the zipper to the notch marking the top of the pleat, reinforcing the ends with backstitch, but leaving the rest of the seam just basted in place. From the WS, press the seam allowance open, as well as the wider pleat extension pieces at the base of the seam. With WS uppermost, center the closed zipper over the seam allowance, with the reverse of the zipper facing upward and the end stopper lined up with the hemline of the top.

7 On the RS of the garment, topstitch ⑯ along each side of the zipper, parallel to the center seam and around 1/4 in. (6 mm) away from it (depending on the width of the zipper selvedge edges). Be careful to keep the seam running straight as you go past the zipper pull.

8 With the back section WS uppermost, place the underlay over the pleat extension section RS down, extending the edge 5/8 in. (15 mm) above the top of the pleat. Pin and baste ⑦ the underlay to each side of the pleat section only. Stitch the seams and press.

9 Pin and baste ⑦ across the top of the pleat. Turn the back section over, and stitch a triangle with the base across the top of the pleat and through the layers of back, pleat extensions, and the pleat underlay, with the point upward and centered on the center back seam.

10 Place the front and back sections RS together, matching all notches, and pin, then baste ⑦ in place. Stitch the side seams, then the shoulder seam. From the WS, press the seams open then turn the garment RS out.

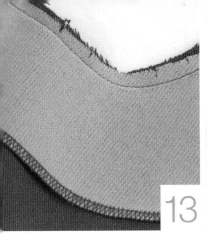

11 Place the interfacing on the WS of one piece of back neckline facing and baste ⑦ in place. Repeat for the other back neckline facing and the front neckline facing.

12 Stitch the front and back neckline facings at the shoulder seams. Trim the interfacing close to the seam and, from the WS, press the seams flat. Turn under 1/4 in. (6 mm) along the ends and the outer curved edge of the facing and press. Stitch along the curved edge to hold the folded edge in place.

13 With the dress RS out, place the neckline facing RS together on top, lining up center back, notches, and the neck edges. Pin then baste ⑦ in place. Stitch the neckline facing to the garment all round the neckline.

14 Fold the neckline facing through the neck of the dress to the inside, so it covers the raw edges of the neck. Slipstitch ⑭ at the shoulder seams and down the sides at the zipper to hold in place.

15 With RS together, stitch one set of front and back armhole facings together at the underarm seam and the shoulder seam. From the WS, press the seams open. Turn under 1/4 in. (6 mm) along the outer curved edge of the facing and press. Stitch along the curved edge to hold the folded edge in place.

16 With the garment RS outward, pin the armhole facing around the armhole, matching seams and notches. Baste ⑦ in position, then stitch with the machine.

17 Turn the armhole facing through the armhole to the inside and, from the WS, press into place. Slipstitch ⑭ at the seams to hold in position. Repeat steps 14–16 for the other armhole.

18 Try on the dress and measure the correct length. Turn up the hem once along the hemline, then turn under the raw edge by 1/4 in. (6 mm) to neaten, and pin in place. Hem ⑫ around to hold in place.

Finishing

Remove all basting threads. Neaten any loose thread ends by either sewing them in or snipping them close to the stitching. Press the garment.

> **TIP**
> - *This dress is designed to be knee-length. If you want to make it longer, add length to the pattern pieces at the hem before cutting. Remember that you will also need to lengthen the pleat underlay by the same amount.*

Drawstring Top

This easy-sew hooded top is spot on for playful kids! The contrasting fabrics and detailing add visual interest, while an adjustable drawstring around the waist makes it oh-so-comfy all day long.

Pattern pieces

A. Front—place center front line to a fold, cut one in fabric color 1

B. Front yoke—cut two in fabric color 1 and two in fabric color 2

C. Back—place center back line to a fold, cut one in fabric color 1

D. Hood—cut two in fabric color 1 and two in fabric color 2

E. Back neck facing—place center back line to a fold, cut one in fabric color 2

F. Armhole binding—cut 2 on the bias in fabric color 2.

G. Pocket—cut two in fabric color 2

Suitable fabrics

Knitted cotton, jersey, fleece, brushed cotton, fine wool, corduroy

Notions

Sewing thread to match fabric

One snap fastener or button

Bias binding to match fabric
    (optional)

1 yd. (1 m) of thin ribbon or cord

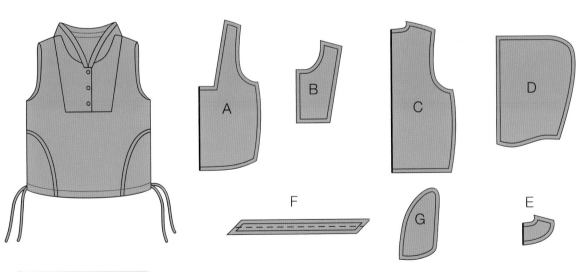

These templates can be found on the CD-Rom

4

7

14

1 Line up the pattern pieces on the straight of grain of the fabric ① and pin them in position ②. Cut out all the pattern pieces ③ as listed and mark notches ④.

2 Run a line of stay-stitching ⑥ along the curved edges of the front and back sections and around the top of the hood and the pocket to keep the edges stable and stop them stretching as you work.

3 Place two matching front yoke pieces RS together, pin and baste ⑦ in position around the top and the front edge that will overlap. Machine-stitch from the notch marking the start of the hood to the corner, swivel the needle in the fabric at the corner, then stitch down the front edge. Trim seams, clip across the corner, clip into the seam allowance to the stitching line at the notch at the start of the hood, being careful not to cut through the stitching. Turn yoke RS out. Repeat for the other yoke section.

4 Place the left front yoke and the front RS together, matching raw edges, pin and baste ⑦ in position around the yoke side and bottom edges. Position the other yoke section on the other side in the same way, so the two yokes overlap at center front. Machine-stitch the yoke into the front along sides and bottom. From the WS, press the seams away from the yoke.

5 Fold over the seam allowance on the curved edge of one of the pocket pieces, clip ⑪ into the curved edge along the seam allowance—being careful not to cut over the stitching line—then press the seam allowance flat.

6 Fold over the fabric by 1/8 in (3 mm) twice within the seam allowance on the opening edge of the pocket and press flat. Topstitch ⑯ the fold in place.

7 Place the patch pocket in position on the front of the garment, matching marks, and pin in place, then baste ⑦. Topstitch ⑯ along the curved edge through only the front of the top and the pocket. Repeat steps 5–7 for the other pocket.

8 Place the front and back RS together, baste ⑦, and then stitch the side seams to within 1 in. (2.5 cm) of the hemline, then from the hemline to the bottom edge, being careful not to catch the open edges of the pockets as you sew. From the WS, press the seams open then turn the garment RS out. The slits left in the seams at each side will be the openings for the drawstrings.

9 Place the two hood pieces in color 1 RS together, pin and baste ⑦ in position, then stitch together from the top front to the center back around the curved edge. Clip the curves ⑪ and press the seam as flat as possible. Repeat with the other two hood pieces in color 2.

16

Place the hood in color 1 RS together to the top, matching notches all around the neckline. Pin and baste ⑦ in position. Machine-stitch around the neckline.

11 Place the hood in color 2 RS together to the back neck facing, matching center back line, all notches, and with neck edges in line. Machine-stitch the two together. Turn under 1/4 in. (6 mm) along the raw edges of the back neck facing and press in position. Run a line of machine stitching along the fold to keep it in position. Alternatively, you can finish the raw edges with zigzag stitching.

12 Place this second hood over the first hood already attached to the rest of the top, RS together. Pin and baste ⑦ in position. Machine-stitch around the edges of the hood. Turn the second hood inside out to line the first hood, folding the back neck facing inside the back of the top. Slipstitch ⑭ at the shoulder seams to hold in place.

13 With the garment RS outward, pin the armhole binding around the armhole, RS together. Baste ⑦ in position, lapping the raw edges over at the end. Tuck under the end that will show on the RS to neaten it, then machine-stitch the binding in place.

14 Fold the binding over to the inside, enclosing the raw edges of the armhole. Ease any

creases, tuck the raw edge of the binding under, pin and baste ⑦ in position. Hem ⑫ around the armhole on the inside to keep the binding in place. Repeat steps 13–14 for the other armhole.

15 Turn up the hem once along the hemline by 5/8 in. (15 mm) to make a channel for the drawstring, then turn under the raw edge to neaten it and pin in place. Hem ⑫ around to hold in place.

16 Alternatively, cut separate front and back contrast edging strips, fold the short ends under to neaten, then stitch one long side around the hem RS together. Fold over to the inside and slipstitch in place. The gap between the two strips allows access for the drawstring.

17 Use a bodkin—a needle with a very large eye to take wide ribbon or string—to thread the drawstrings through from each side, or pin a large safety pin to one end instead. Thread the ends of the drawstring into the channels around the hem and use your fingers to ease the bodkin or safety pin all through the channels.

18 When both ends of each drawstring are protruding on each side of the hem, adjust them to an equal length on both sides. Finish the ends of the drawstring with a neat knot, or add a bought toggle end.

19 Add a snap fastener to the overlap of the yoke at the neck, with the corresponding half on the underlap beneath.

Finishing

Remove all basting threads. Neaten any loose thread ends by either sewing them in or snipping them close to the stitching. Press the garment.

Flared Skirt

Circular skirts are easy to make, and they hang beautifully—this one is only a half circle, but the fabric still drapes into graceful folds. You can use a large print as long as it does not have an obvious direction because the design will run vertically at the front but horizontally at the seam.

Pattern pieces

A. Skirt—cut one in fabric

B. Waistband—place center front line to a fold, cut one in fabric, one in interfacing

Suitable fabrics

Cotton, polycotton, denim, satin, silk

Notions

Sewing thread to match fabric

Interfacing for waistband

9 in. (22 cm) zipper

2 snap fasteners

Bias binding (optional)

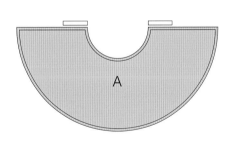

A

B

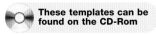

These templates can be found on the CD-Rom

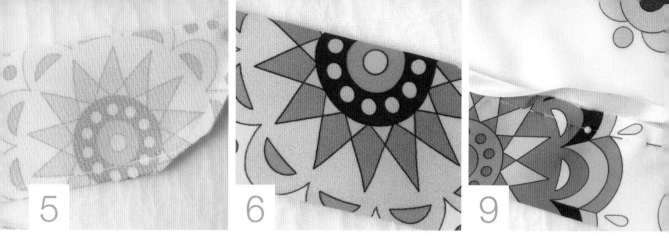

1 Line up the pattern pieces on the straight of grain of the fabric ① and pin them in position ②. Cut out all the pattern pieces ③ as listed and mark notches ④ and the position of any dots or markings ⑤.

2 Run a line of stay-stitching ⑥ along the curved edges of the skirt to keep the edge stable and stop it stretching as you work.

3 Fold the skirt around RS together and line up the center back seam. Baste ⑦ the center back seam then machine-stitch from the notch marking the end of the zipper to the bottom of the skirt, leaving the rest of the seam just basted in place. From the WS press the seam allowance open. With WS uppermost, center the closed zipper over the seam allowance, with the reverse of the zipper facing upward and the end stopper lined up with the hemline of the top.

4 On the RS of the garment, topstitch ⑯ along each side of the zipper, parallel to the center seam and around 1/4 in. (6 mm) away from it (depending on the width of the zipper selvedge edges). Be careful to keep the seam running straight as you go past the zipper pull.

5 Place the strip of interfacing on the WS of the waistband. Baste ⑦ the interfacing in position with large stitches that will be easy to remove later.

6 With RS together, fold the waistband lengthwise along the centerline. Stitch across one short end, and across and down the long seam by only 1 in. (2.5 cm) at the other end for the overlap section.

7 Turn the waistband RS out, pushing out the corners gently into a point with a blunt point.

8 Place one side of the waistband section RS together to the top edge of the skirt, matching center back line, all notches, and the raw edges and baste ⑦ in place. Stitch the waistband to the skirt. Trim the seam allowances to 3/8 in. (9 mm) and press toward the waistband.

9 Fold the waistband over to enclose the raw edges of the waistline. Tuck the waistband seam allowance under and stitch into place with slipstitch ⑭, being careful not to go through to the RS of the fabric. Alternatively, enclose the inside raw edge of the waistband with a strip of bias binding and then machine-stitch through binding, waistband, and skirt. Make sure this new line of stitching runs along the join between waistband and skirt on the RS, so it will be almost invisible when the skirt is worn.

10 Mark the position of the machine-stitched buttonhole ⑰ in the waistband overlap and work it, either following the instructions with your sewing machine or as described on page 23.

12

11 Overlap the buttonhole over the underlap of the waistband and push a pin through the end of the buttonhole to mark where the button should go. Stitch the button ⑳ in place.

12 Try on the skirt and mark the hem. To make a baby hem, machine-stitch $1/8$ in. (3 mm) from the raw edge all around the hem on the RS. Press the fabric under along the stitching line, so the raw edge points upward on the WS. On the RS, machine-stitch $1/8$ in. (3 mm) in from the edge of the fold all around again. Press under along the new stitching line; the raw edge on the WS is now enclosed. Tug gently on the seam to ease it. On the RS, topstitch ⑯ very close to the edge of the hem all around to hold all the folds on the WS in place.

Finishing

Remove all basting threads. Neaten any loose thread ends by either sewing them in or snipping them close to the stitching. Press the garment.

TIP

• *When turning up the hem on the circular skirt, make sure that it is very narrow, as the flare of the skirt will mean that the folded and turned-up edge of the hem will be much longer than the line along which it is being sewn. The narrower the hem, the smaller the difference will be, so the hem will be easier to sew.*

Vest

The choice of fabric for this simple vest will totally change its look—make it in pinstripe for a tailored effect or in broderie anglaise to bring out your gypsy style. It can be worn open or buttoned at the front.

Pattern pieces

A. Front—cut two in fabric

B. Front facing—cut two in fabric, two in interfacing

C. Back—cut two in fabric

D. Back neck facing—cut two in fabric, two in interfacing

E. Front armhole facing—cut one in fabric, one in interfacing

F. Back armhole facing—cut one in fabric, one in interfacing

Suitable fabrics

Denim, cotton, gabardine, wool, velvet, corduroy

Notions

Sewing thread to match fabric

Interfacing for facings

Four buttons

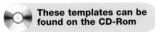
These templates can be found on the CD-Rom

14 15 20

1 Line up the pattern pieces on the straight of grain of the fabric ① and pin them in position ②. Cut out all the pattern pieces ③ as listed and mark notches ④ and the position of darts ⑤.

2 Run a line of stay-stitching ⑥ along the curved edges of all the front and back sections to keep the edges stable and prevent them stretching.

3 Fold the front side section along the centerline of the long dart and pin. Baste ⑦ along the sewing line of the dart then stitch the double-ended dart, working from center to point in each direction.

4 Repeat step 3 for the other double-ended dart. On the WS, press the darts flat toward the side seams.

5 Stitch the two bust darts in the same way, stitching from the edge of the fabric to the point of the dart.

6 Place the two back sections RS together and pin and baste ⑦ together, then stitch. Place the back and front sections RS together, pin andbaste ⑦ together at the side and shoulder seams. Stitch the seams and press open from the WS.

7 Place the interfacing on the WS of one of the back neck facings, matching notches, and baste ⑦ in place. Repeat for the other back neck facing and the front facings.

8 Stitch the two halves of the back neck facing together. Stitch the back facing to the front facings at the shoulder seams. Trim the interfacing close to the seam and, from the WS, press the seams flat. Either finish the raw edges with zigzag stitch or turn under a small hem of 1/4 in. (6 mm) and machine-stitch in place.

9 With the vest RS out place the facing on top, RS together, with raw edges aligned around the neckline and down the front opening and matching center back and shoulder seams. Pin then baste ⑦ in place. Stitch the facing to the garment front starting at one bottom edge, up one front side, round the neckline, down the other front side, and across the other bottom edge.

10 Fold the facing through to the inside of the vest so it covers the raw edges of the seam you have just made.

11 With RS together, stitch one set of front and back armhole facings together at the underarm seam and the shoulder seam. From the WS, press the seams open. Either finish the raw edges with zigzag stitch or turn under a small hem of 1/4 in. (6 mm) and machine-stitch in place.

12 With the garment RS outward, pin the armhole facing around the armhole, matching seams and notches. Baste ⑦ in position, then stitch with the machine.

13 Turn the armhole facing through the armhole to the inside and from the WS press into place. Slipstitch ⑭ at the seams to hold in position. Repeat steps 17–19 for the other armhole.

14 Turn up the hem by 5/8 in. (15 mm) along the hemline, then turn under the raw edge to neaten it and pin in place.

15 Either hem ⑫ around to hold in place, or run a line of topstitching ⑯ all around the base of the vest to finish the hem.

16 Mark the position of the buttonholes ⑲ on the overlap of the front. Remember that women's garments cross right over left.

17 With small stitches machine a rectangle 1/8 in. (3 mm) around the buttonhole position line. Slash along the position line through both front and front facing and oversew the raw edges.

18 A horizontal buttonhole has fanned stitches at the end toward the open edge. With the fanned edge of the buttonhole to the right, fasten matching buttonhole thread to the bottom left corner, then working from left to right, insert the needle through the slash to the RS, just outside the line of machine stitching. Loop the thread under the

point and the eye of the needle. Pull the needle to form a small knot at the cut edge—this is known as buttonhole stitch.

19 Working stitches close together, continue along the edge. At the end, fan the stitches, then turn around and work along the other edge.

20 At the final end, work a bar tack of several stitches across the two rows of buttonhole stitches, then fasten off.

21 Overlap the buttonhole over the underlap side of the vest and push a pin through the end of the buttonhole to mark where the button should go. Stitch the buttons ⑳ in place.

Finishing

Remove all basting threads. Neaten any loose thread ends by either sewing them in or snipping them close to the stitching. Press the garment.

3

Sleeves, collars, and pockets

Learn to create sleeves, collars, and cuffs, and add new skills to your repertoire. The tailored blouse is a timeless classic while the relaxed tunic makes a fashion staple. A pretty tulip skirt paired with a lacy blouse is perfect for a night on the town.

Tailored Blouse

This open-neck blouse teaches you how to make a tailored collar—which is simpler to work in a lighter fabric but can also be used on a coat or jacket. The main seams are done as French seams, which gives a couture look and is ideal for very light fabrics.

Pattern pieces

A. Center front—cut four in fabric, two in interfacing

B. Side front—cut two in fabric

C. Side back—cut two in fabric

D. Center back—place center back line to a fold, cut one in fabric

E. Sleeve—cut two in fabric

F. Back neck facing—place center back line to a fold, cut one in fabric, one in interfacing

G. Collar—place center back line to a fold, cut two in fabric, one in interfacing

Suitable fabrics

Medium- or lightweight cotton, cotton lawn, polycotton, polyester, fine wool

Notions

Sewing thread to match fabric

Interfacing for collar and facings

Four buttons

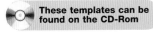
These templates can be found on the CD-Rom

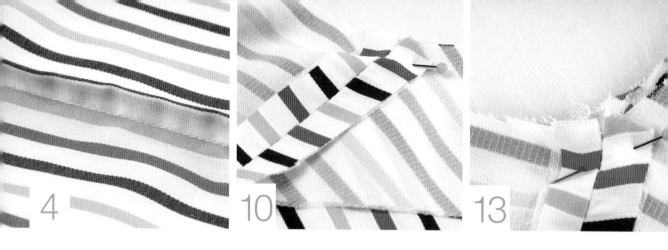

4

10

13

1 Line up the pattern pieces on the straight of grain of the fabric ① and pin them in position ②. Cut out all the pattern pieces ③ as listed and mark notches ④ and the position of darts ⑤.

2 Run a line of stay-stitching ⑥ along the curved edges of the front and back sections and around the top of the sleeves to keep the edges stable and stop them stretching as you work.

3 Stitch the princess seam, which runs down the front from shoulder to hem with a French seam as follows: place the front and one side front WRONG SIDES together and stitch only 1/2 in. (12 mm) from the edge. Trim the seam allowance to a scant 1/8 in. (3 mm) and press open.

4 Fold the fabric RS together along the stitching line you have just made. Stitch a second seam on the seam line, enclosing the raw edges of the fabric. From the WS, press the seam to one side.

5 Repeat steps 3–4 for the other side front and for the back pieces.

6 Stitch the fronts to the back along the side seams, then stitch the shoulder seams, using a French seam   as described in steps 3–4. From the WS, press the seams to one side.

7 Place the two collar pieces RS together and place the interfacing on top, baste ⑦ in position, then stitch through all three layers along the seam line of one end, around the outside of the collar, and down the other end. Leave the neck edge open. Trim the seam allowances back and snip diagonally across the corners, being careful not to cut through the line of stitching. Turn the collar RS outward, pushing out all points gently with a blunt end and press.

8 Of the four center front pieces, two will be the front of the blouse and two will be front facings. Place the interfacing on the WS of one front facing and baste ⑦ in position using large stitches. Repeat on the other front facing and the back neck facing.

9 Baste ⑦ one front facing to the end of the back neck facing at the top, then stitch in place. Repeat for the other front facing. Trim the interfacing close to the seam line. Either finish the raw edges with zigzag stitch or turn under by 1/4 in. (6 mm) and machine-stitch in place.

10 Pin the interfaced side of the collar RS together to the neckline of the blouse, matching the center back line, all notches, and edges. Then place the facing on top, RS downward, matching the edges down the center fronts and around the neckline. Stitch in position through all layers. Trim close to the seam line and clip all curved edges. From the WS, press the seams toward the facing.

11 Turn the facing to the inside of the garment, pushing out all points gently with a blunt end, and press in position.

12 Stitch the dart in the elbow of the sleeve. Stitch the sleeve seam with a French seam , as described in steps 3–4, to make a tube of fabric. From the WS, press the seam to one side.

13 Turn the sleeve RS out and turn the garment inside out. Slip the sleeve inside the armhole and pin them together at the sleeve and garment underarm seams, shoulder markings, and notches. Baste ⑦ into place, then stitch on the machine with sleeve side up, being careful not to pull the fabric.

14 To reinforce the seam under the arm, stitch a second line of reinforcement stitching ⑧ inside the first, within the seam allowance.

15 Trim the seam close to the stitching and clip curves ⑪, then zigzag or overcast the edges. Turn up the bottom of the sleeve and hem ⑫ in place. Repeat steps 12–15 for the other sleeve.

16 Mark the position of the machine-stitched buttonholes ⑰ and work them either following the instructions with your sewing machine or as described on page 23.

17 Stitch on the buttons ⑳ to match the positions of the buttonholes. Turn up the hemline to a suitable length, turn under the raw edge, and hem ⑫ in place.

Finishing

Remove all basting threads. Neaten any loose thread ends by either sewing them in or snipping them close to the stitching. Press the garment.

Child's Dress

This charming child's dress has been made shorter to wear as a top. It has a pretty rounded collar and a button front—the button opening at the neck is called a placket and a different version of the same feature is used at the cuff.

Pattern pieces

A. Back—place center back line to a fold, cut one in fabric

B. Front—cut two in fabric

C. Sleeve—cut two in fabric

D. Cuff—cut two in fabric, two in interfacing

E. Collar—place center back line to a fold, cut two in fabric, one in interfacing

F. Neckline placket band—cut two in fabric, two in interfacing

G. Back neck facing—place center back line to a fold, cut one in fabric, one in interfacing

H. Pocket—cut two in fabric

I. Cuff placket band—cut two in fabric

Suitable fabrics

Medium- or lightweight cotton, cotton lawn, polycotton, denim, fine wool, velvet

Notions

Sewing thread to match fabric

Interfacing for collar, cuffs and facings

Six buttons

Six snap fasteners

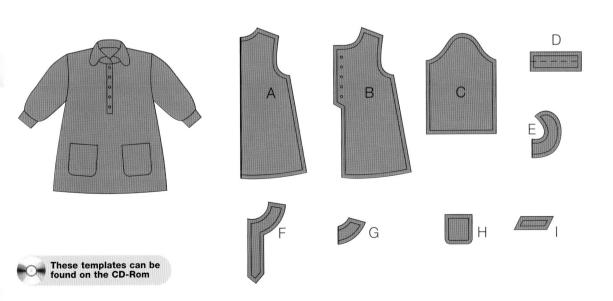

These templates can be found on the CD-Rom

1 Line up the pattern pieces on the straight of grain of the fabric ① and pin them in position ②. Cut out all the pattern pieces ③ as listed and mark notches ④.

2 Run a line of stay-stitching ⑥ along the curved edges of the front and back sections and around the top of the sleeves to keep the edges stable and stop them stretching as you work.

3 Place the two front sections RS together and baste ⑦ in place. Stitch as far as the bottom of the front neck opening. From the WS, press the seam open.

4 Fold over the seam allowance around the sides and bottom of one of the pocket pieces, clip ⑪ into the curved edge along the seam allowance, being careful not to cut over the stitching line, then press the seam allowance flat.

5 Fold over the fabric twice within the seam allowance on the opening edge of the pocket and press it flat. Topstitch ⑯ the fold in place.

6 Place the patch pocket in position on the front of the garment and pin in place, then baste ⑦. Topstitch ⑯ along one side, across the bottom, and up the other side of the pocket. Repeat steps 4–6 for the other pocket.

7 Stitch the fronts to the back along the side seams, then stitch the shoulder seams. From the WS, press the seams to one side.

8 Place the two collar pieces RS together and place the interfacing on top, baste ⑦ in position, then stitch through all three layers along the seam line of one end, around the outside of the collar, and

down the other end. Leave the neck edge open. Trim the seam allowances back and clip ⑪ curved edges, being careful not to cut through the line of stitching. Turn the collar RS outward and press.

9 Place the interfacing on the WS of one neckline placket band, matching notches, and baste ⑦ in position using large stitches. Repeat on the other neckline placket band and also on the back neck facing.

10 Baste ⑦ one neckline placket band to the end of the back neck facing at the top, then stitch in place. Repeat for the other neckline placket band. Trim the interfacing close to the seam line.

11 Pin the interfaced side of the collar RS together to the neckline of the dress, matching the center back line, all notches, and edges.

12 Place the facing on top, RS downward, matching the center back and the edges down the center fronts and around the neckline. Stitch in position through all layers, being careful not to stitch the two halves of the front together.

13 Trim close to the seam line and clip all curved edges. From the WS, press the seams toward the facing. Turn the facing to the inside of the garment, pushing out all points gently with a blunt end, and press in position.

14 Fold the sleeve in half lengthwise, RS together and stitch the sleeve seam to make a tube of fabric. From the WS, press the seam to one side.

15 Turn the sleeve RS out and turn the garment inside out. Slip the sleeve inside the armhole and pin them together at the sleeve and garment

underarm seams, shoulder markings, and notches. Baste ⑦ into place, then stitch on the machine with the sleeve side up and being careful not to pull the fabric as you work.

16 To reinforce the seam under the arm, stitch a second line of reinforcement stitching ⑧ inside the first, within the seam allowance.

17 Trim the seam allowance close to the stitching and clip curves ⑪, then zigzag or overcast the edges. Repeat steps 14–17 for the other sleeve.

18 On the cuff end of the sleeve, stitch a V-shape line of reinforcement ⑧ stitching up and down on either side of the marked slash line. Snip to the slash line to the end, without cutting through the stitches.

19 Spread the edges of the opening apart so they almost form a straight line. With RS together, pin the cuff placket band to the opening edge. Stitch ¹⁄₄ in. (6 mm) away from the edge, using small stitches. Trim one of the edges back a little and press the seam allowances toward the placket band.

20 Press under ¹⁄₄ in. (6 mm) along the remaining raw edge of the cuff placket band. Pin the fold over the seam on the inside of the sleeve and slipstitch ⑭ in place.

TIPS

- *This dress has been made quite short to wear as a top over pants, but you can make it normal length. To check the length roughly before you begin, measure the back pattern piece against the back of a dress the correct length—but remember it should be longer to allow for turning up the hem.*

- *Small children find buttons difficult so here they are just for decoration and the front and cuff close with snap fasteners beneath.*

21 Fold the placket band down in the center and press to one side. Stitch a diagonal line across the top of the fold to hold it in place.

22 Fold the cuff in half lengthwise RS together and place the interfacing on top, baste ⑦ in position then stitch through all three layers along the seam line of one end, around the outside of the cuff, and down the other end. Leave the sleeve edge open. Trim the seam allowances back and snip diagonally across the corners, being careful not to cut through the line of stitching. Turn the cuff RS outward and press.

23 Run a double line of gathering ⑨ stitches around the end of the sleeve, from one edge of the placket band to the other. Gather the end of the sleeve to fit the cuff.

24 Place the interfaced side of the cuff RS together to the end of the sleeve, matching notches and the ends. Baste ⑦ then stitch in place, stitching with the gathered sleeve uppermost to avoid pulling the gathers.

25 Fold the cuff over the raw edges of the seam you have just made, turn the seam allowance under, and slipstitch ⑭ in place on the inside. Repeat steps 18–25 on the other sleeve.

26 Stitch four buttons ⑳ in a line on the placket band, spaced equally apart. Stitch a button to the overlap of each cuff. Matching the positions of the buttons, stitch a snap fastener beneath each to hold the openings closed.

27 Turn up the hemline to a suitable length, turn under the raw edge, and hem ⑫ in place.

Finishing

Remove all basting threads. Neaten any loose thread ends by either sewing them in or snipping them close to the stitching. Press the garment.

Swing Jacket

Designs can be made to look very different just by changing or extending one detail. This stylish swing-back jacket has short sleeves and a shawl collar that is cut as one with the front, and can run right to the hem or be folded back at a higher level.

Pattern pieces

A. Front—cut two in fabric

B. Back—place center back line to a fold, cut one in fabric

C. Sleeve—cut two in fabric

D. Front facing—cut two in fabric, two in interfacing

E. Back neck facing—place center back line to a fold, cut one in fabric, one in interfacing

F. Pocket—cut two in fabric

Suitable fabrics

Medium- or lightweight cotton, brushed cotton, polycotton, jersey, fine wool, lightweight needle cord

Notions

Sewing thread to match fabric

Interfacing for front and collar

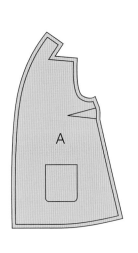

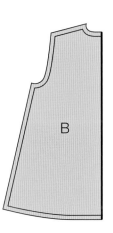

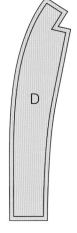

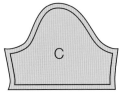

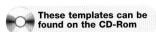
These templates can be found on the CD-Rom

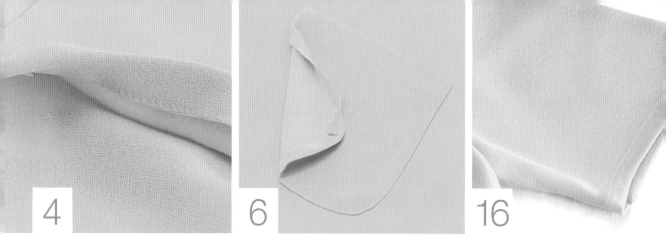

1 Line up the pattern pieces on the straight of grain of the fabric ① and pin them in position ②. Cut out all the pattern pieces ③ as listed and mark notches ④ and the position of darts ⑤.

2 Run a line of stay-stitching ⑥ along the curved edges of the front and back sections and around the top of the sleeves to keep the edges stable and stop them stretching as you work.

3 Stitch the bust dart on one front section. Place the front RS together to the back, matching notches along the side seams, baste ⑦, then stitch. Repeat with the shoulder seam. From the WS, press seams open. Repeat step ③ for the other front section.

4 Fold over the seam allowance around the sides and bottom of one pocket piece, clip ⑪ into the curved edge along the seam allowance, being careful not to cut over the stitching line, then press the seam allowance flat.

5 Fold over the fabric twice within the seam allowance on the opening edge of the pocket and press it flat. Topstitch ⑯ the fold in place.

6 Place the patch pocket in position on the front of the garment and pin in place, then baste ⑦. Topstitch ⑯ along one side, across the bottom, and up the other side of the pocket. Repeat steps 4–6 for the other pocket.

7 Place the interfacing on the WS of one front facing and baste ⑦ in position using large stitches. Repeat on the other front facing and also on the back neck facing.

8 Baste ⑦ one front facing to the end of the back neck facing at the short edge, then stitch in place. Repeat for the other front facing. Trim the interfacing close to the seam line.

9 Pin the facing to the jacket neckline and front edges, RS downward, matching the center back line, notches, and all edges. Stitch in position through all layers. Trim close to the seam line and clip all curved edges. From the WS, press the seams toward the facing.

10 Turn the facing to the inside of the garment and press in position. Finish the raw edgings of the facings with zigzag stitching or by folding the raw edges under by 1/4 in. (6 mm) and machine-stitch in place.

11 Fold the sleeve in half lengthwise, RS together, and stitch the sleeve seam to make a tube of fabric. From the WS, press the seam to one side.

12 Turn the sleeve RS out and turn the garment inside out. Slip the sleeve inside the armhole and pin them together at the sleeve and garment underarm seams, shoulder markings, and notches.

Baste ⑦ into place, then stitch on the machine with the sleeve side up and being careful not to pull the fabric as you work.

14 To reinforce the seam under the arm, stitch a second line of reinforcement stitching ⑧ inside the first, within the seam allowance.

15 Trim the seam allowance close to the stitching and clip curves ⑪, then zigzag or overcast the edges.

16 Try on the jacket and turn the sleeve under to a suitable length, turn the raw edge under to neaten, and hem ⑫ in place. Repeat steps 11–16 for the other sleeve.

17 Turn up the hemline to a suitable length, turn the raw edge under to neaten, and hem ⑫ in place.

Finishing

Remove all basting threads. Neaten any loose thread ends by either sewing them in or snipping them close to the stitching. Press the garment.

> **TIP**
> • *The jacket has no fastenings, but you could add two or three large buttons down the front if you wish.*

Tulip Skirt

This knee-length tulip skirt works from day to night without missing a beat. Not only are pleats used to fit fabric round the curves of the body, here they are also a design feature that accentuates the curved shape of a garment.

Pattern pieces

A. Front—place center front to a fold, cut one in fabric

B. Back—cut two in fabric

C. Waistband—place center front to a fold, cut one in fabric, one in interfacing

Suitable fabrics

Medium- or lightweight cotton or linen, polycotton, gabardine, fine wool

Notions

Sewing thread to match fabric

One 1/2 in (13mm) button

One 9 in. (22 cm) zipper

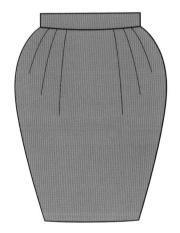

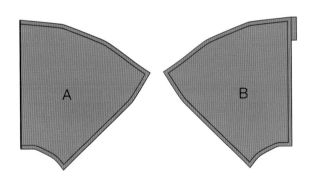

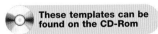

These templates can be found on the CD-Rom

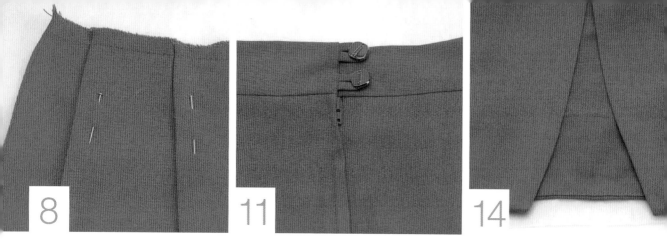

1 Line up the pattern pieces on the straight of grain of the fabric ① and pin them in position ②. Cut out all the pattern pieces ③ as listed and mark notches ④ and the position of pleats.

2 Run a line of stay-stitching ⑥ along the curved edges of the skirt to keep the edge stable and stop it stretching as you work.

3 Place the two back pieces of the skirt RS together and line up the center back seam. Baste ⑦ the center back seam then, leaving the top of the seam basted in place, machine-stitch from the notch marking the end of the zipper to the bottom of the skirt, leaving the last 4 in. (10 cm) at the hem unstitched. This will leave room to walk in the skirt, as the hem is quite narrow.

4 From the WS, press the seam allowance open. With WS uppermost, center the closed zipper over the seam allowance, with the reverse of the zipper facing upward and the end stopper lined up with the hemline of the top.

5 On the RS of the garment, topstitch ⑯ along each side of the zipper, parallel to the center seam and around 1/4 in. (6 mm) away from it (depending on the width of the zipper selvedge edges). Be careful to keep the seam running straight as you go past the zipper pull.

6 Stitch the front and the back of the skirt together along both side seams. From the WS, press the seams open.

7 Place the strip of interfacing on the WS of the waistband. Baste ⑦ the interfacing in position with large stitches that will be easy to remove later.

8 Fold the pleats in the top of the skirt and baste ⑦ into position.

9 Place one side of the waistband section RS together to the top edge of the skirt, matching center back line, all notches, and raw edges, and baste ⑦ in place. Stitch the waistband to the skirt. Trim the seam allowances trim to 3/8 in. (9 mm) and press toward the waistband.

10 To make the button loops, cut a strip of spare fabric 1 in. (2.5cm) wide and 4 in. (10 cm) long. Fold this piece lengthwise RS together and stitch 1/4 in. (6 mm) away from the raw edges. Trim the raw edges close to the seam then turn the tube of fabric you have made RS out and cut in half. Curve the two tubes into two equal loops big enough to go over your buttons and position them on the overlap end of the waistband so the raw ends of the loops are lining up with the raw edge of the overlap and the loops are pointing toward the main section of waistband. Baste ⑦ the loops in position along the seam line.

11 With RS together, fold the waistband lengthwise along the centerline and stitch across the overlap end, through both layers and through the ends of the button loops. On the underlap, turn the waistband seam allowance down then stitch from the fold across the end, pivot at the corner, and stitch to the end of the underlap, being careful not to catch the skirt. Trim the seam allowance. Turn the overlap and underlap RS out—the loops should now protrude from the end of the waistband overlap.

12 Fold the central section of the waistband over to enclose all the raw edges, tuck the seam allowance under, and stitch into place with slipstitch ⑭, being careful not to go through to the right side of the fabric.

13 Overlap the button loops over the underlap of the waistband and push a pin through the center of the loop to mark where the button should go. Stitch the button ⑳ in place.

14 Try on the skirt and turn up along the hemline to a suitable length around the bottom of the skirt. Turn under the raw edge and hem ⑫ in position, easing any excess fabric as required to keep the hem as flat as possible. Slipstitch ⑭ the seam allowance flat on either side of the slit in the bottom of the back seam.

Finishing

Remove all basting threads. Neaten any loose thread ends by either sewing them in or snipping them close to the stitching. Press the garment.

Hooded Top

Athletic wear never looked so good! Sleeves that join to a top in a diagonal line from neck to underarm are called raglan sleeves. They're much easier to set, or stitch in place, than normal sleeves.

Pattern pieces

A. Front—place center front line to a fold, cut one in fabric

B. Front yoke—cut two in fabric

C. Back—place center back line to a fold, cut one in fabric

D. Hood—cut four in fabric

E. Sleeve—cut two in fabric

F. Pocket—cut four in fabric

G. Pocket welt band—cut two in fabric

H. Back neck facing—place center back line to a fold, cut one in fabric, one in interfacing

I. Front neck facing—cut two in fabric, two in interfacing

Suitable fabrics

Fleece, jersey, brushed cotton, denim, corduroy

Notions

Sewing thread to match fabric

Two toggle ends for drawstrings (optional)

One 5 in. (12 cm) zipper

Interfacing for the facings

1 yd. (1 m) of thin cord for the drawstring

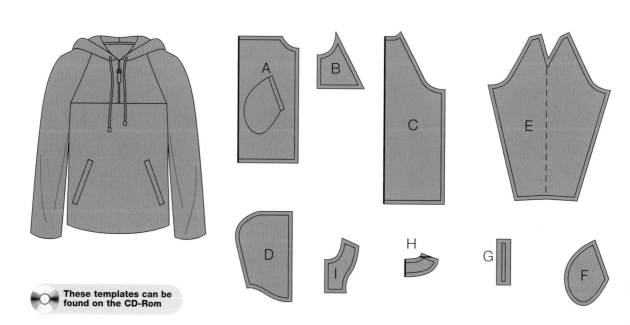

These templates can be found on the CD-Rom

10　　　13　　　14

1 Line up the pattern pieces on the straight of grain of the fabric ① and pin them in position ②. Cut out all the pattern pieces ③ as listed and mark notches ④.

2 Run a line of stay-stitching ⑥ along the curved edges of the front and back sections and around the top of the hood and the pocket to keep the edges stable and stop them stretching as you work.

3 Place the two yoke pieces RS together, lining up the center front seam. Baste ⑦ the center front seam then press the seam open from the WS.

4 With RS together, stitch the yoke to the top of the front section. From the WS, press the seams away from the yoke.

5 With WS uppermost, center the closed zipper over the seam allowance, with the reverse of the zipper facing upward and the end stopper lined up with end of the opening in the yoke.

6 On the RS of the garment, topstitch ⑯ along each side of the zipper, parallel to the center seam and around 1/4 in. (6 mm) away from it (depending on the width of the zipper selvedge edges). Be careful to keep the seam running straight as you go past the zipper pull.

7 Carefully mark the diagonal position of the welt pocket opening on each side of the front on the RS with a rectangle of basting ⑦ where you want the welt band to fall.

8 Fold the pocket welt band in half lengthwise, RS together, and press. Stitch the ends, trim the seam allowance, and clip corners diagonally, then turn RS out and press.

9 Pin the welt band over the lower line of one of the marked rectangles, on the RS of the front section. The raw edges of the welt band should point uppermost and the seam line of the welt band should fall over the lower line of the rectangle.

10 Place one of the pocket pieces over the welt band, RS down, with the seam line on the straight edge falling over the seam line of the welt band. Place the mirror-image pocket piece above the first, RS down, with the seam line on the straight edge falling over the upper line of the rectangle.

11 Stitch the upper line of the rectangle through the pocket piece and the lower line through the other pocket piece and the welt band. Backstitch at each end of the line with small stitches.

12 Slash along the centerline of the rectangle lengthwise to within 1/2 in. (12 mm) of the ends, then clip diagonally into the corners. Turn the

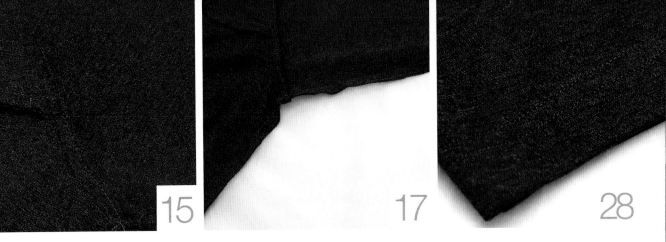

15

17

28

two pocket pieces to the inside and pull on the triangular ends to square the corners. Turn up the welt and press.

13 Matching the pocket edges as much as possible, pin together then stitch, taking care to catch the base of the triangles in the stitching. Trim the seam allowances and finish all the raw edges.

14 On the RS, slipstitch ⑭ the ends of the welt in place. Repeat steps 8–14 for the other pocket.

15 Place the front and one sleeve RS together and stitch the raglan seams. Run a second line of stitching around ¼ in. (6 mm) away from the first, near the raw edges. Repeat for the other sleeve.

16 Repeat step 15 on the back section and the sleeve.

17 Place the front and back RS together, folding the sleeve over RS together as well. Baste ⑦ into place, then stitch on the machine from the bottom of the garment, up under the arm, and down to the end of the sleeve in one continuous seam.

18 To reinforce the seam under the arm, stitch a second line of reinforcement stitching ⑧ inside the first, within the seam allowance.

19 Trim the seam allowance close to the stitching and clip curves ⑪, then zigzag or overcast the edges. Turn up the bottom of the sleeve and hem ⑫ in place. Repeat steps 17–19 for the other sleeve.

20 Place two hood pieces RS together, pin and baste ⑦ in position, then stitch together from the top front to the center back around the curved edge. Clip the curves ⑪ and press the seam as flat as possible. Repeat with the other two hood pieces.

21 Place one hood section RS together to the neckline, matching notches, pin and baste ⑦ in position. Machine-stitch around the neckline.

22 Place one front neck facing and the back neck facing RS together, lining up the shoulder seam. Stitch together, then repeat for the other front neck facing. Fold back the seam allowance on the center front edges and press in place. Either finish the raw edges with zigzag stitch or turn them under and machine-stitch in place.

23 Place the second hood RS together to the neck facing, matching center back line, all notches, and with neck edges in line. Machine-stitch the two together, leaving a small gap in the seam at the front of the hood on each side to allow access for the drawstring.

24 Place the second hood over the first hood already attached to the rest of the top, RS together. Pin and baste ⑦ in position. Machine-stitch around the edges of the hood. Turn the second hood inside out to line the first hood, folding the back neck facing inside the back of the top.

25 Stitch around the front of the hood about 1/2 in. (12 mm) from the edge to create a defined channel for the drawstring. Make sure the channel begins and ends at the gap you left in the seam in step 23.

26 Remove the basting at the zipper and open it. Fold the neck facing down so it covers the raw edges at the back of the garment and slipstitch ⑭ at the shoulder seams and down each side of the zipper to hold in place.

27 Turn up the hem along the hemline and hem ⑫ in place.

28 Add a line of decorative topstitching in a contrasting thread around the sleeve ends and just above the line of the hem.

29 Use a bodkin—a needle with a very large eye to take wide ribbon or string—to thread the drawstring, or pin a large safety pin to one end instead. Thread the end of the drawstring into the channel around the hood and use your fingers to ease the bodkin or safety pin all through the channel.

30 When both ends of the drawstring are protruding, adjust to an equal length on both sides. Finish the ends of the drawstring with a neat knot, or add a purchased toggle end, following the manufacturer's instructions.

Finishing

Remove all basting threads. Neaten any loose thread ends by either sewing them in or snipping them close to the stitching. Press the garment.

TIPS

- *The zipper and the topstitching can be in a contrasting or matching color.*

- *If you cannot find a short enough zipper, buy a longer one and shorten it by stitching firmly across the teeth so the pull can only so far.*

Tie-front Tunic

A pretty bow lends a touch of femininity to this easy-going design. The tunic includes simple patch pockets, but these can be omitted for a smooth look.

Pattern pieces

A. Front—place center front line to a fold, cut one in fabric

B. Back—place center back line to a fold, cut one in fabric

C. Sleeve—cut two in fabric

D. Pocket—cut two in fabric

E. Collar/neck tie—cut one in fabric

F. Back neck facing—place center back line to a fold, cut one in fabric, one in interfacing

G. Front neck facing—place center front line to a fold, cut one in fabric, one in interfacing

Suitable fabrics

Light- or medium-weight cotton, cotton lawn, silk, velvet, fine wool

Notions

Sewing thread to match fabric

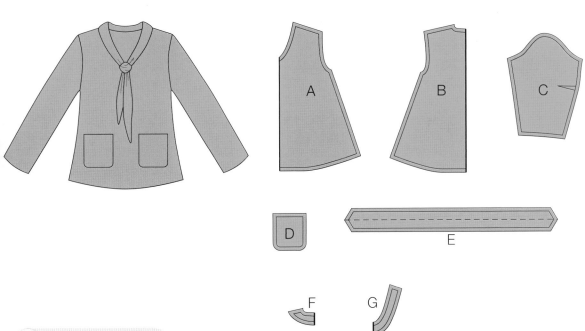

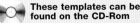

These templates can be found on the CD-Rom

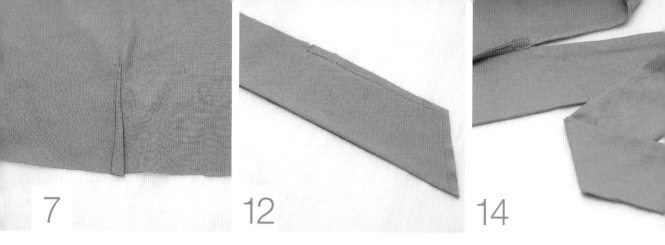

7   **12**   **14**

1 Line up the pattern pieces on the straight of grain of the fabric ① and pin them in position ②. Cut out all the pattern pieces ③ as listed and mark notches ④ and the position of darts ⑤.

2 Run a line of stay-stitching ⑥ along the curved edges of the front and back sections and around the top of the sleeves to keep the edges stable.

3 Fold over the seam allowance around the sides and bottom of one of the pocket pieces, clip ⑪ into the curved edge along the seam allowance—being careful not to cut over the stitching line—then press the seam allowance flat.

4 Fold over the fabric twice within the seam allowance on the opening edge of the pocket and press it flat. Topstitch ⑯ the fold in place.

5 Place the patch pocket in position on the front of the garment and pin in place, then baste ⑦. Topstitch ⑯ along one side, across the bottom, and up the other side of the pocket. Repeat steps 3–5 for the other pocket.

6 Place the front and back RS together, pin in place, then stitch the side and shoulder seams.

7 Stitch the dart in the elbow of the sleeve. Stitch the sleeve seam to make a tube of fabric. From the WS, press the seam to one side.

8 Turn the sleeve RS out and turn the garment inside out. Slip the sleeve inside the armhole and pin them together at the sleeve and garment underarm seams, shoulder markings, and notches. Baste ⑦ into place, then stitch on the machine with the sleeve side up, being careful not to pull the fabric as you work.

9 To reinforce the seam under the arm, stitch a second line of reinforcement stitching ⑧ inside the first, within the seam allowance.

10 Trim the seam allowance close to the stitching and clip curves ⑪, then zigzag or overcast the edges. Turn up the bottom of the sleeve and hem ⑫ in place. Repeat steps 12–15 for the other sleeve.

11 Fold the neck tie in half along the length, RS together, and press.

12 Stitch each tie end from the dots marking the ends of the collar. DO NOT stitch the collar section. Snip diagonally across the two corners at each end of the ties, to reduce the bulk of the seam, being very careful not to cut through the stitching.

13 Turn the tie sections RS out, pushing out the corners gently from the inside with a blunt point, such as a knitting needle, to get a nice sharp corner.

14 Place the collar section RS together to the top edge of the blouse, matching center back line, all notches, and edges, and baste ⑦ in place.

15 Stitch the front neck facing to the back neck facing at both shoulder seams. Place the completed neck facing RS down on top of the collar layer, lining up the center back line, center front line, shoulder seams, and neck edges. Pin then baste ⑦ in position. Sew around the neck seam, through all three layers of fabric, being careful not to catch the ties.

16 Fold the neck facing to the inside so it covers the raw edges at the neckline of the garment and slipstitch ⑭ at the shoulder seams to hold in place. Either finish the raw edges with zigzag stitch or fold under and machine-stitch in place.

17 Turn up the hemline to a suitable length, turn under the raw edges, and hem ⑫ in place.

Finishing

Remove all basting threads. Neaten any loose thread ends by either sewing them in or snipping them close to the stitching. Press the garment.

4

Tailoring techniques

This chapter is all about tailoring techniques and covers those finishing touches that will make your garment look more sophisticated and professional. As well as a pair of smart trousers there are three different jackets—one with lining—and a smart unisex rain cape.

Jeans

These stylish jeans are made in a smart khaki cotton. For a more traditional jeans look try chambray, which is a blue denim-look fabric that is softer and easier to work than true denim. The jean-style stitching on the pockets is very easy to achieve.

Pattern pieces

A. Trouser front—cut two in fabric

B. Trouser back—cut two in fabric

C. Back yoke—cut two in fabric

D. Back pocket—cut two in fabric

E. Front pocket lining—cut two in lining

F. Front pocket back—cut two in fabric

G. Waistband—place center back line to a fold, cut one in fabric, one in interfacing

Suitable fabrics

Chambray, lightweight denim, cotton drill, heavyweight cotton, linen

Notions

Sewing thread to match fabric

Contrast thread (optional)

Interfacing for waistband

One button

One 7 in. (18 cm) zipper

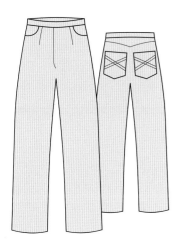
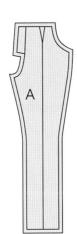
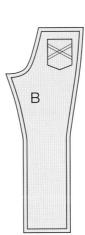
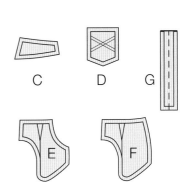

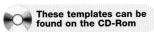

These templates can be found on the CD-Rom

4

6

10

1 Line up the pattern pieces on the straight of grain of the fabric ① and pin them in position ②. Cut out all the pattern pieces ③ as listed and mark notches ④ and the position of darts ⑤.

2 Run a line of stay-stitching ⑥ along the curved edges of the crotch on all four main sections and on the pocket pieces to keep the edges stable and stop them stretching as you work.

3 Stitch the darts at the waist. Place the two front sections RS together, matching notches, and baste ⑦ in place. Stitch the center front seam to the bottom end of where the zipper will finish, backstitching at the end to keep the seam secure.

4 Fold both extensions to the inside along fold lines, and baste ⑦ close to the edges. Place the closed zipper under the left front, the teeth close to the folded edge, baste ⑦ in place, then stitch around 1/8 in. (3 mm) away from the teeth.

5 Matching center front markings, lap the right-hand edge over the zipper and baste ⑦ in place through all thicknesses close to the fold.

6 From the inside, baste ⑦ the zipper along the stitching line, through all layers. On the outside of the right front, topstitch through all layers along the basted markings, curving round at the bottom to the base of the zipper. Pull threads to the WS and tie.

7 Make a series of little clips ⑪ into the seam allowance on the curved crotch seam, being very careful not to cut into the stitching. Space them about 1 in. (2.5 cm) apart, so that the curved seam will lie flat. From the WS, press the seams open.

8 With RS together and lining up markings and edges, place the front pocket lining over the matching front section and baste ⑦ in place. Stitch the front pocket lining to the garment. Trim seam allowances to different lengths to grade the seam, clip the curve, and press the seam open, then press the seam allowance toward the lining.

9 Fold the front pocket lining to the inside, press in place, then topstitch ⑯ along the pocket edge to hold it in place.

10 With RS together, pin the front pocket back to the front pocket lining and baste ⑦ in place. Stitch the front pocket back to the front pocket lining. Press and then zigzag along the raw edges. Baste ⑦ the front pocket to the garment at the top and along the side below the pocket opening. Repeat steps 8–10 for the other front pocket.

11 Place the two back sections RS together, matching notches, and baste ⑦. Stitch the center back seam. Clip ⑪ into the seam allowance on the curved crotch seam, being careful not to cut the stitching. From the WS, press seams open.

12 With RS together, stitch the two halves of the yoke together. The yoke is sewn to the top of the trouser back with a flat fell seam. Pin the yoke and back WRONG SIDES together, matching notches, then baste ⑦. Using a contrast thread in the machine, stitch the side seam only 1/2 in. (12 mm) from the edge. Trim the seam allowance to a scant 1/8 in. (3 mm) and press open.

13 Turn under 1/4 in. (6 mm) of the top seam allowance and baste ⑦ in place on the RS of the garment over the trimmed edge. Still with the contrast thread in the machine, edge stitch close to the fold, through the seam allowance and garment.

14 Fold over the seam allowance around the sides and bottom of one of the back pocket pieces, clip ⑪ into the pointed edge along the seam allowance, being careful not to cut over the stitching line, then press the seam allowance flat.

15 Fold over the fabric twice within the seam allowance on the opening edge of the pocket and press it flat. Topstitch ⑯ the fold in place.

16 Make the decorative lines of stitching on the pocket, using the contrast thread.

17 Place the back pocket in position on the back of the garment and pin in place, then baste ⑦. Topstitch ⑯ along one side, across the

TIPS

- *The instructions for the fly front zipper are for a placket crossing from right to left for women's trousers. If you are making the trousers for a man, read "right" for "left" and vice versa so the zipper will cross from left to right.*

- *The flat fell seam is stitched in contrasting thread, as it is on jeans, but you can use a matching color if you prefer.*

bottom, and up the other side of the pocket. Repeat steps 13–16 for the other pocket.

18 The back and front sections are again stitched together with a flat fell seam. Pin the back and front WRONG SIDES together, matching notches. Follow the instructions for a flat fell seam in steps 12–13. Repeat on the other side.

19 Place the interfacing on the WS of the waistband and baste ⑦ in place with long stitches that will be easy to remove later.

20 Place one side of the waistband section RS together to the top edge of the trousers, matching raw edges and notches and baste ⑦ in place. Stitch the waistband to the trousers. Trim the seam allowances trim to ³/₈ in. (9 mm) and press toward the waistband.

21 With RS together, fold the waistband lengthwise along the center line and stitch across the overlap end. On the underlap, turn the waistband seam allowance down then stitch from the fold across the end, pivot at the corner, and stitch to the end of the underlap, being careful not to catch the trousers. Trim the seam allowance.

22 Fold the other side of the waistband over the seam you have just made, enclosing all the raw edges, tuck the seam allowance under, and stitch into place with slipstitch ⑭, being careful not to go through to the RS of the fabric.

23 Mark the position of the machine-stitched buttonhole ⑰ in the overlap of the waistband and work it either following the instructions with your sewing machine or as described on page 23.

24 Overlap the buttonhole over the underlap of the waistband and push a pin through the end of the buttonhole to mark where the button should go. Stitch the button ⑳ in place.

25 Try the trousers on to check the length before turning the hem, or measure them against an existing pair the right length. Pin the hem in place and try them on again to check the length is correct. Turn the raw edge under again by ¹/₄ in. (6 mm) before hemming ⑫ round each leg end.

Finishing

Remove all basting threads. Neaten any loose thread ends by either sewing them in or snipping them close to the stitching. Press the garment.

All-weather Cape

A unisex cape is a great alternative to a coat or jacket and this one is nice and roomy to wear over thicker winter clothes. The front pouch pocket could be omitted to create a simpler version.

Pattern pieces

A. Front—place center front line to a fold, cut one in fabric

B. Yoke—cut two in fabric

C. Back—place center back line to a fold, cut one in fabric

D. Hood side—cut two in fabric

E. Hood center—cut one in fabric

F. Hood peak—cut two in fabric, one in interfacing

G. Hood lining—cut two in fabric

H. Sleeve—cut two in fabric

I. Cuff—cut two in fabric, two in interfacing

J. Front pocket flap—place center front line to a fold, cut one in fabric

K. Front pocket—place center front line to a fold, cut one in fabric

L. Strap fasteners—cut four in fabric, two in interfacing

Suitable fabrics

Waterproofed cotton, nylon, waxed cotton, gabardine

Notions

Sewing thread to match fabric

Strip of hook-and-loop tape

One 10 in. (26 cm) zipper, or zipper tape cut to length and stitched across the teeth as a stopper

Interfacing for peak and straps

Stiffening for peak (optional)

Bias binding (optional)

Two medium buttons

Two large buttons or hook-and-loop tab squares

Four eyelet holes (optional)

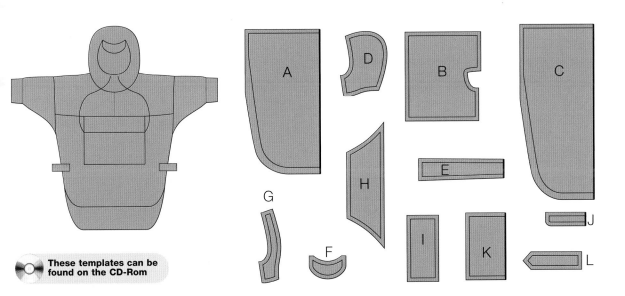

These templates can be found on the CD-Rom

1 Line up the pattern pieces on the straight of grain of the fabric ① and pin them in position ②. Cut out all the pattern pieces ③ as listed and mark notches ④.

2 If the fabric stretches, run a line of stay-stitching ⑥ along the curved edges of the front and back sections and around the top of the hood and the pocket to keep the edges stable and stop them stretching as you work.

3 Place the two back yoke pieces RS together, pin and baste ⑦ in position down the center back line, then stitch together.

4 Place one side hood piece RS together to the center hood, pin and baste ⑦ in position, then stitch together from the top front to the center back around the curved edge. Repeat for the other side of the hood. Clip the curves ⑪ and press the seam as flat as possible.

5 Place the two hood peak pieces RS together, add the interfacing to the top, baste ⑦ around three sides, then stitch. Grade the seam allowance by trimming the pieces to different lengths and clip diagonally across the points, being careful not to cut the stitching. Turn RS out and press. Topstitch ⑯ around the three stitched sides.

6 Stitch the two pieces of the hood lining together at the top front seam, press the seam open. Place the raw edge of the peak RS together to the raw edge of the front of the hood. Place the hood lining RS together on top, lining up any marks and notches. Pin and baste ⑦ in position, then sew around the front edge of the hood.

7 Turn the lining to the inside of the hood, so the peak juts out at the front, and topstitch ⑯ around the hood opening to hold everything in position. Turn the raw edges of the hood lining under by 1/4 in. (6 mm), press and machine-stitch in position.

8 Place the hood and the garment yoke RS together, with neck edges in line. Pin then baste ⑦ in position. Sew around the neck seam, through all layers of fabric.

9 Pin and baste ⑦ the front seam RS together up the center front of the yoke and the center front of the hood. Press the seam open.

10 With WS uppermost, center the closed zipper over the seam allowance down the center of the front yoke and hood, with the reverse of the zipper facing upward and the end stopper lined up with the bottom of the opening in the yoke.

11 On the RS of the garment, topstitch ⑯ along each side of the zipper, parallel to the center seam and around 1/4 in. (6 mm) away from it (depending on the width of the zipper selvedge edges). Be careful to keep the seam running straight as you go past the zipper pull.

12 Run another line of topstitching from the zipper to the shoulder seam edge, just above the bottom of the yoke, catching the seam allowance.

13 Place the two pocket flap pieces RS together, baste ⑦ around three sides, then stitch. Grade the seam allowance by trimming the two pieces to different lengths and clip diagonally across the points, being careful not to cut the stitching. Turn RS out and press. Topstitch ⑯ around the three stitched sides.

14 Place pocket flap on the bottom, with the front RS down on top and the yoke WS on top of that, aligning the raw edges and making sure the pocket flap is centered on both the yoke and the front section. Pin and baste ⑦ through all layers. Machine-stitch through the three layers of yoke, pocket flap, and front section only 1/2 in. (12 mm) from the edge.

15 Fold the front section and the pocket flap down and trim the underneath seam allowance to a scant 1/8 in. (3 mm). Turn under 1/4 in. (6 mm) of the top seam allowance and baste ⑦ in place on the RS of the garment over the trimmed edge. Edge stitch close to the fold, through the yoke, pocket flap, and front. You have now made a flat fell seam across the front, holding the pocket flap in place.

16 Fold over the seam allowance on the sides and bottom edge of the pocket piece, then press the seam allowances flat.

17 Fold over the fabric twice within the seam allowance on the opening edge of the pocket and press it flat. Topstitch ⑯ the fold in place.

18 Place the patch pocket in position on the garment front under the pocket flap and pin in place, then baste ⑦. Topstitch ⑯ along the sides and bottom through the front and the pocket.

19 Place the back and the back yoke WS together and join with a flat fell seam as described on page 27.

20 Fold the sleeve in half lengthwise, WS together, and stitch the sleeve seam with a flat fell seam to make a tube of fabric.

21 Turn the sleeve RS out and turn the garment inside out. Slip the sleeve inside the armhole and pin them together at the sleeve and garment underarm seams, shoulder markings, and notches. Baste ⑦ into place, then stitch on the machine with the sleeve side up, being careful not to pull the fabric as you work.

22 To reinforce the seam under the arm, stitch a second line of reinforcement stitching ⑧ inside the first, within the seam allowance.

23 Trim the seam allowance close to the stitching and clip curves ⑪, then zigzag or overcast the edges.

24 Place the interfacing on the WS of the cuff piece and tack ⑦ in place. With RS together, fold the cuff widthwise and stitch together across the short end. Trim the interfacing back to the stitching line and press the seam open.

31

32

25 Place the cuff piece over the sleeve end, RS together, matching raw edges and notches, and baste ⑦ in place. Stitch the cuff to the sleeve. Trim the seam allowances to ³/₈ in. (9mm) and press toward the cuff.

26 Fold the cuff over lengthwise, WS together, along the center line, enclosing the raw edges of the seam you have just made. Tuck under the seam allowance on the inside of the cuff and stitch into place with slipstitch ⑭, being careful not to go through to the RS of the fabric. Repeat steps 24–26 for the other sleeve.

27 If you are using fabric that frays, you will need to bind the edges. Open out one folded edge of a length of bias binding and pin right around the bottom edges of the front. Baste ⑦ in place down the fold line. Fold the bias binding round to the back, enclosing the raw edges of the fabric, and baste ⑦ in place. Machine-stitch all round over the bias binding, being careful to catch it in on both sides as you go. Repeat for the back. If your fabric does not fray, you can just fold the fabric edge to the inside by around ¼ in. (6 mm), pin in place at intervals, then run a double line of topstitching ⑯ all around.

28 Place two of the strap fastener pieces RS together, add a layer of interfacing on the top, and stitch round three sides. Trim the seams and

turn RS out. Turn in the seam allowance at the opening and top stitch around all four sides.

29 Stitch one end of the strap fastener to the outside seam of the back piece as indicated on the pattern. Mark the position of the machine-stitched buttonhole ⑰ at the end of the strap and work it either following the instructions with your sewing machine or as described on page 23. Stitch the large button ⑳ in place in a corresponding position on the front of the cape. Repeat steps 28–29 for the other strap fastener.

30 Alternatively, you can sew square hook-and-loop tabs on the strap and the front of the cape. Stitch a strip of hook-and-loop tabs on the underside of the pocket flap and a matching strip on the top of the pocket.

31 Insert two eyelets just below the armhole on each side of front and back, following the manufacturer's instructions.

Finishing

Remove all basting threads. Neaten any loose thread ends by either sewing them in or snipping them close to the stitching. Press the garment.

Asymmetric-front Jacket

This jacket is based on an ordinary double-breasted jacket pattern, but has no collar and the front is an unusual asymmetrical cut fastened with a single decorative button. The internal seams are bound with contrasting fabric, which is a neat finish for an unlined jacket.

Pattern pieces

A. Front—cut four in fabric, two in interfacing

B. Side front—cut two in fabric

C. Side back—cut two in fabric

D. Back—cut two in fabric

E. Sleeve—cut two in fabric

F. Back neck facing—place center back line to a fold, cut one in fabric, one in interfacing

Suitable fabrics

Wool, gabardine, denim, heavyweight cotton, linen

Notions

Sewing thread to match fabric

Interfacing for front

One decorative button

One plain button

Contrast seam binding (optional)

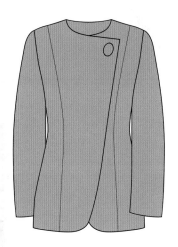

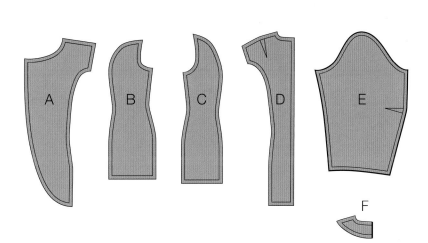

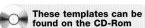

These templates can be found on the CD-Rom

1 Line up the pattern pieces on the straight of grain of the fabric ① and pin them in position ②. Cut out all the pattern pieces ③ as listed and mark notches ④ and the position of darts ⑤.

2 Run a line of stay-stitching ⑥ along the curved edges of the front and back sections and around the top of the sleeves to keep the edges stable and stop them stretching as you work.

3 Of the four front pieces, two will be the front of the jacket and two will be front facings. Place one of the fronts and one side front RS together along the front seam curving from hem to armhole, matching notches, and baste ⑦ in place then stitch. Repeat for the other side and for the back sections.

4 Place the front sections RS together to the back, matching notches along the side seams, and baste ⑦ then stitch. Repeat with the shoulder seams.

5 Stitch the dart in the elbow of the sleeve. Baste ⑦ then stitch the sleeve seam to make a tube of fabric. From the WS, press the seam open.

6 Turn the sleeve RS out and turn the garment inside out. Slip the sleeve inside the armhole and pin them together at the sleeve and garment underarm seams, shoulder markings, and notches. Baste ⑦ into place, then stitch on the machine with the sleeve side up, being careful not to pull the fabric as you work.

7 To reinforce the seam under the arm, stitch a second line of reinforcement stitching ⑧ inside the first, within the seam allowance. Trim the seam allowance close to the stitching and clip curves ⑪, then zigzag or overcast the edges. Repeat steps 5–7 for the other sleeve.

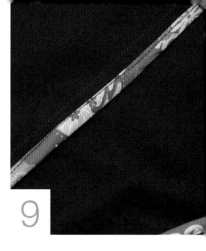

9

8 The inside seams of this jacket are finished with contrast binding, which can either be cut from another fabric or purchased bias binding. If you use another fabric, cut strips 1 in. (2.5 cm) on the bias, then fold the edges under by 1/4 in. (6 mm) on each side and press.

9 Do not press the seams open. Fold the contrast bias tape over both raw edges, baste ⑦, then machine-stitch to hold in place along the seam.

10 Mark the position of the bound buttonhole at the top over the overlap front. Cut a rectangular patch of fabric 1 in. (2.5 cm) wide and 1 in. (2.5 cm) longer than the finished buttonhole. With WS together, fold the long edges so the raw edges meet in the center.

11 With the cut edges facing up, center the patch over the buttonhole marking on the RS. Baste ⑦ through the center. Using small stitches, start at the center of one lip and stitch a rectangular box around the buttonhole marking, working the same number of stitches across each end and pivoting at the corners. Do not finish with backstitches but pull the ends to the WS and tie off.

12 Remove the basting and slash through the center of the patch and the garment, between the rows of stitching clipping diagonally into the corners. There are two methods of slashing

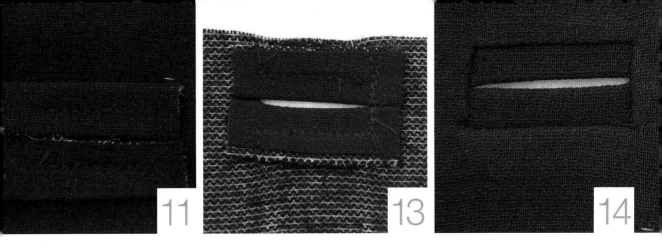

the opening. Either cut along the center to within 1/4 in. (6 mm) of each end, then clip diagonally into the corners. Alternatively, for fabrics that fray, cut from the center diagonally into each corner. NB With either method, take care NOT to cut the stitches.

13 Turn the patch through to the WS and press. Baste ⑦ the folds together across the center.

14 With the garment RS up, fold the garment back and stitch back and forth over the little triangles at each end to make a neat rectangle on the front. Trim the patch to 1/4 in. (6 mm) from the stitching line. Turn the garment RS out again and press with a cloth protecting the buttonhole. Repeat steps 10–14 to make a second buttonhole in a corresponding position on the underlap front.

15 Place the interfacing on the WS of one front facing and baste ⑦ in position using large stitches. Repeat on the other front facing and also on the back neck facing.

16 Baste ⑦ one front facing to the end of the back neck facing at the shoulder seam, then stitch in place. Repeat for the other front facing. Trim the interfacing close to the seam line. Either finish the raw edges with bias binding as described in steps 8–9 or turn the raw edges under by 1/4 in. (6 mm) and machine-stitch to hold in place.

17 Turn the jacket RS out. Pin the facing RS together to the neckline and front edges of the jacket, matching the center back line, all notches, and center front edges. Stitch in position through all layers. Trim close to the seam line and clip all curved edges. From the WS, press the seams toward the facing.

18 Turn the facing to the inside, pushing out all points gently with a blunt end, and press.

19 With the facing flat in position underneath, push a pin through each corner of the buttonhole. Turn the front over and slash the facing along the centerline of the buttonhole and clip diagonally into the corners. Turn the raw edges under and slipstitch opening ⑭ them in place. Repeat for the other bound buttonhole. Slipstitch the facing at the shoulder seams and at intervals down the front to hold in place.

20 Stitch on the buttons ⑳ to match the positions of the buttonholes.

21 Turn up the bottom of the sleeves and the jacket hemline to a suitable length. Turn the raw edge under by 1/4 in. (6 mm) hem ⑫ in place.

Finishing

Remove all basting threads. Neaten any loose thread ends by either sewing them in or snipping them close to the stitching. Press the garment.

Double-breasted Cropped Jacket

Double-breasted jackets are made in the same way as a normal jacket, but with wrap-over front panels. The stand-up, or mandarin, collar gives this one a smart military look.

Pattern pieces

A. Front—cut four in fabric, two in interfacing

B. Side front—cut two in fabric

C. Side back—cut two in fabric

D. Back—cut two in fabric

E. Collar—place center back line to a fold, cut one in fabric, one in interfacing

F. Sleeve—cut two in fabric

G. Back neck facing—place center back line to a fold, cut one in fabric, one in interfacing

Suitable fabrics

Wool, gabardine, heavyweight cotton, cotton drill, linen, denim

Notions

Sewing thread to match fabric
Interfacing for front and collar and back neck facing
Eight decorative buttons
One large press stud

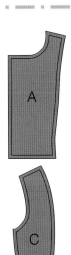

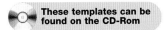
These templates can be found on the CD-Rom

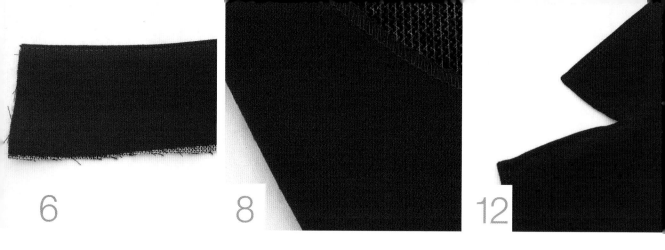

6

8

12

1 Line up the pattern pieces on the straight of grain of the fabric ① and pin them in position ②. Cut out all the pattern pieces ③ as listed and mark notches ④ and the position of darts ⑤.

2 Run a line of stay-stitching ⑥ along the curved edges of the front and back sections and around the top of the sleeves to keep the edges stable and stop them stretching as you work.

3 Of the four front pieces, two are the front of the jacket and the other two are the front facings. Place the front and one side front RS together down the front seam from shoulder to hem, matching notches and raw edges. Baste ⑦ in position then stitch. Finish the raw edges of the seam allowance with zigzag stitch or oversewing and press open. Repeat for the other side of the front.

4 Stitch the two halves of the back RS together, then place the back and one side back RS together down the seam from shoulder to hem, matching notches and raw edges. Baste ⑦ in position then stitch. Finish the seam allowance as before and press open. Repeat for the other side of the back.

5 Stitch the fronts to the back along the side seams as above, then stitch the shoulder seams. From the WS, press the seams open.

6 Place the two collar pieces RS together and place the interfacing on top, baste ⑦ in position then stitch through all three layers along the seam line of one end, around the outside of the collar and down the other end. Leave the neck edge open. Trim the seam allowances and snip diagonally across corners. Turn the collar RS outward and press.

7 Place the interfacing on the WS of one front facing and baste ⑦ in position using large stitches. Repeat on the other front facing and the back neck facing.

8 Baste ⑦ one front facing to the end of the back neck facing at the shoulder seam, then stitch in place. Repeat for the other front facing. Trim the interfacing close to the seam line. Turn the raw edges of the facing under by 1/4 in. (6 mm), press, and machine-stitch in position, or overlock the edges.

9 Pin the interfaced side of the collar RS together to the neckline of the jacket, matching the center back line, all notches, and edges. Then place the facing on top, RS downward, matching the center back line, edges down the jacket fronts, and around the neckline. Stitch in position through all layers. Trim close to the seam line and clip all curved edges. From the WS, press the seams toward the facing.

6

TIP

- *This jacket is cut so the hem falls just below the waistline. Lengthen the main pattern pieces A, B, C, and D before you pin and cut if you want it longer.*

10 Turn the facing to the inside of the garment, pushing out all points gently with a blunt end, and press in position.

11 Stitch the dart in the elbow of the sleeve. Pin or baste ⑦, then stitch the sleeve seam to make a tube of fabric. From the WS, press the seam to one side.

12 Turn the sleeve RS out and turn the garment inside out. Slip the sleeve inside the armhole and pin them together at the sleeve and garment underarm seams, shoulder markings, and notches. Baste ⑦ into place, then stitch on the machine with the sleeve side up, being careful not to pull the fabric as you work.

13 To reinforce the seam under the arm, stitch a second line of reinforcement stitching ⑧ inside the first, within the seam allowance.

14 Trim the seam allowance close to the stitching and clip curves ⑪, then zigzag or oversew the edges. Turn up the bottom of the sleeve and hem ⑫ in place. Repeat steps 11–14 for the other sleeve.

15 Mark the position of the machine-stitched buttonholes ⑰ down the front overlap and work them either following the instructions with your sewing machine or as described on page 23.

16 Stitch on the buttons ⑳ to match the positions of the buttonholes, plus a matching line of buttons on the opposite side of the overlapping edge. Add a large press stud under the top button of the opposite side to hold the underlap front in place.

17 Turn up the jacket hemline, turn the raw edge under again by 1/4 in. (6 mm), and hem ⑫ in place.

Finishing

Remove all basting threads. Neaten any loose thread ends by either sewing them in or snipping them close to the stitching. Press the garment.

Shawl-collared Jacket

Lining your projects not only hides the construction seams inside but also makes them hang better and prolongs their life. This project features a two-part sleeve for a more fitted and tailored look.

Pattern pieces

A. Front—cut four in fabric, two in interfacing

B. Side front—cut two in fabric, two in lining

C. Side back—cut two in fabric, two in lining

D. Back—cut two in fabric, two in lining

E. Top front sleeve—cut two in fabric, two in lining

F. Back sleeve—cut two in fabric, two in lining

G. Bottom pocket—cut two in fabric, two in lining

H. Bottom pocket welt—cut two in fabric

Suitable fabrics

Wool, gabardine, denim, heavyweight cotton, linen, velvet

Notions

Sewing thread to match fabric

Interlining for front and back collar

Lining fabric—quantity to match main fabric

Five buttons

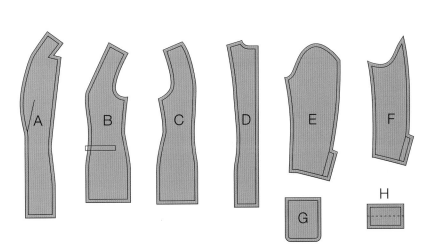

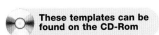
These templates can be found on the CD-Rom

1 Line up the pattern pieces on the straight of grain of the fabric ① and pin them in position ②. Cut out all the pattern pieces ③ as listed and mark notches ④.

2 Run a line of stay-stitching ⑥ along the curved edges of the front and back sections and around the top of the sleeves to keep the edges stable and stop them stretching as you work.

3 Of the four front pieces, two are the front of the jacket and the other two are the front facings. Place a front and one side front RS together along the princess seam from hem to shoulder and baste ⑦ in place, then stitch the seam. Press the seam allowance open. Repeat for the other side front.

4 Repeat step 3 for the back pieces, then pin and stitch the two halves of the back together.

5 Place the fronts RS together to the back, matching notches along the side seams, and baste ⑦ then stitch. Repeat with the shoulder seams. From the WS, press the seams open.

6 Repeat steps 4–5 for the lining pieces. At the center back, make a small pleat in the lining at top and bottom and stitch into place.

7 Carefully mark the position of the bottom welt pocket opening on each side of the front on the RS with a rectangle of basting ⑦ where you want the welt band to fall.

8 Fold the bottom pocket welt band in half lengthwise, RS together, and press. Stitch the ends, trim the seam allowance, and clip corners diagonally, then turn RS out and press.

9 Pin the bottom welt band over the lower line of one of the marked rectangles, on the RS of the front section. The raw edges of the welt band should point uppermost and the seamline of the welt band should fall over the lower line of the rectangle.

10 Place one of the pocket lining pieces over the welt band, RS down, with the seamline on the straight edge falling over the seamline of the welt band. Place one of the pocket pieces above this, RS down, with the seamline on the straight edge falling over the upper line of the rectangle.

11 Stitch the upper line of the rectangle through the pocket piece and the lower line through the pocket lining and the welt band. Backstitch at each end of the line with small stitches.

12 Slash along the center line of the rectangle lengthwise to within 1/2 in. (12 mm) of the ends, then clip diagonally into the corners. Turn the pocket lining and pocket piece to the inside and pull on the triangular ends to square the corners. Turn up the welt and press.

13 Matching the pocket and pocket lining edges as much as possible, pin together then stitch, taking care to catch the base of the triangles in the stitching. Trim the seam allowances and finish all the raw edges.

14 On the RS, slipstitch ⑭ the ends of the welt down in place. Repeat steps 8–14 for the other pocket.

15 Place the interfacing on the WS of one front facing and baste ⑦ in position using large stitches. Repeat on the other front facing and also on the back neck facing.

6

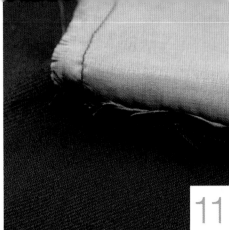

11

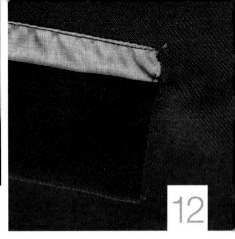

12

16 Baste ⑦ one front facing to the end of the back neck facing at the shoulder seam, then stitch in place. Repeat for the other front facing. Trim the interfacing close to the seam line.

17 Pin the facing to the jacket neckline and front edges, RS downward, matching the center back line, notches, and all edges. Stitch in position through all layers. Trim close to the seam line and clip all curved edges. From the WS, press the seams toward the facing.

18 Turn the facing to the inside of the garment and press in position.

19 Matching notches and raw edges, place the two sections of the sleeve RS together and baste ⑦ in position. Stitch the two pieces of the sleeve together along the front seam and along the back seam as far as the point where the seamline pivots to run across the top of the vent opening at the cuff. Slash diagonally into the seam allowance of the under section from the raw edge to the point where the stitching stops at the top of the vent opening. Press the seams open, running the seam crease continuously down the upper section of vent opening piece only—because of the cut you have made into the seam allowance, you can keep the under section flat to one side, although the seam above the cut is pressed open.

20 Turn the sleeve RS out and turn the garment inside out. Slip the sleeve inside the armhole and pin them together at the sleeve and garment underarm seams, shoulder markings, and notches. Baste ⑦ into place, then stitch on the machine with the sleeve side up, being careful not to pull the fabric as you work.

21 To reinforce the seam under the arm, stitch a second line of reinforcement stitching ⑧ inside the first, within the seam allowance. Trim the seam allowance close to the stitching and clip curves ⑪, then zigzag or overcast the edges.

22 With the sleeve WS out, fold up the hem at the bottom of the sleeve, making a neat miter at the point where the upper section of the vent opening overlaps the hem, and hem ⑫ in place all round, being careful that your stitches do not show on the RS.

23 Wrap the upper section of the vent opening over the under section the depth of the seam allowance, making sure the lower edges are even. Pin in position. Still working on the WS, turn under the raw edge of the under section by 1/4 in. (6 mm) and hem ⑫ in place to the underneath of the upper section. Repeat steps 19–23 for the other sleeve.

18

28

24 The sleeve lining does not need the vent opening, so you can trim off the extending rectangle of fabric at the bottom of the sleeve sections. Matching notches and raw edges, place the two sections of the sleeve lining RS together and baste ⑦ in position. Stitch the two pieces of the sleeve lining together, then insert into the jacket lining as described in steps 20–21.

25 With RS together, pin then baste the lining to the facing, matching the shoulder seams. With the lining side uppermost, and starting at the center back, stitch to twice the depth of the hem from the lower edge. Stitch the other side in the same way.

26 Trim and notch the seam allowances, then press them toward the lining.

27 Turn the lining to the RS, lift up the garment fabric and loosely hand sew the lining to the garment at intervals along the underarm seam.

28 Try on the jacket and turn up the bottom hem to a suitable length, turn under the raw edge by 1/4 in. (6 mm), and hem ⑫ in place. Turn up the lining so it overlaps the top of the jacket hem, then turn under the raw edge by 1/4 in. (6 mm). Hem ⑫ the lining in place along the top of the jacket hem, leaving a fold of loose lining fabric overlapping the hem for ease of wear.

29 Repeat step 28 to finish the bottom of the edge of the sleeves. Sew a button on the overlap, stitching right though all thicknesses of the sleeve. Repeat on the other sleeve.

30 Mark the position of the machine-stitched buttonholes ⑰ down the front overlap and work them either following the instructions with your sewing machine or as described on page 23.

31 Stitch on the buttons ⑳ to match the positions of the buttonholes.

Finishing

Remove all basting threads. Neaten any loose thread ends by either sewing them in or snipping them close to the stitching. Press the garment.

TIPS

- *Making a pleat at the center back of the lining allows the lining to fit inside the jacket, but gives a little ease when the garment is worn.*

- *To line a jacket or skirt, you basically make it again in lining fabric then stitch the lined version inside to cover all seams. Once you have made one and understand the principles, it is easy to work out how to line other projects.*

Sewing supplies

Jo-Ann
www.joann.com

Michaels
www.michaels.com

Software

PatternMaker Software
2643 Seminole Circle
Fairfield, CA 94534-7872
www.patternmaker.com

Acknowledgments

With thanks to Michelle Lo, Katie Hudson and everyone at Collins & Brown for their support, to Kuo Kang Chen and Abby Franklin for the wonderful illustrations, Jeremy Tilston for the great design and Mario Guarino for the stylish photography. Extended gratitude to The Botter and Kim Nish at PatternMaker for all their help, particularly on checking the instructions and making changes to the pattern software. Special thanks to Alice & Co and Emily Theodorou for their great sewing, Cadena for supplying the fabrics and Janome for supplying the sewing machine. To all those who went before; who by choice or by duty put needle to fabric and created beauty.